# The Crystal Skull

# COMPASSION

## Sacred Feminine

Joseph Bennett

The Crystal Skull Compassion

ISBN: 1456588419
ISBN-13 9781456588410

# DEDICATION

This book is dedicated to those people who encouraged me to "take a chance." To those who discouraged me for such a huge leap of faith and later became my supporters. Telling me what they felt from Compassion. To John Swinnerton: "It is better to take a chance than forever feel like you let the opportunity of a life time go by." Especially to Annie, who has stood by me through it all relating to me how Compassion felt and how she wanted things to be.

To my sister Stephanie Bennett who took the fateful photograph that forced me to face this crystal skull of my dreams.

To Cece Stevens for making it possible for Annie and I to attend her Tempe Arizona conference. This made it possible to realize Compassion had her own path to follow in the world of the mainstream world of the crystal skulls.

To Hunbatz Men who explained that Compassion was not a contemporary skull even though found in an import shop.

To Jane Fitzgerald who warned me about my deepest intentions and how they had to be pure and from my heart.

To Carole Davis that showed us Compassion is a crystal skull with something to say. God Bless you all for your insights and wisdom.

The Crystal Skull Compassion

# CONTENTS

## Disclaimer

In my attempt to provide a factual
story of my experience as caretaker
and guardian of the crystal skull
Compassion I have made every effort to
recount events honestly. Any miss-
quotes or conflicting opinions
expressed are the result of my memory.
I am recounting them as I remember
them and are therefore to be taken as
such.

The Crystal Skull Compassion

**ACKNOWLEDGMENTS**


My partner Annie, Stephanie Bennett,
John Swinnerton, Bunny Niewenhous,
Phyllis Wright, Katherine Rosengren,
Hunbarz Men, Carole Wilson/Davis,
Jane Fitzgerald, Mort Murphy,
Gerald Drobesh, James Ziegler,
Megan, Robert Fitzgerald,
Dr. Corbett, Dr. Minch,
Leandro De Souza,
Ziranna, David Shawdowolf,
Philip Coppens, Kathleen McGowan,
Cede Stevens, Marlene Swetlishoff,
Marjorie Harras

FIRST MEETING

Chapter One

There they are again, right on the edge of my consciousness just beyond reach of my focus. Those haunting eyes, emanating a bright white light that has been pursuing me over the past year. They first came to me in my dreams, and now here they are again, in my waking state, as I gasp for breath along a narrow rock trail on Mount Shasta.

I was a career mariner, living on an old sailboat with my college dream girl, Annie. After an epiphany I experienced while sailing up the California coast in 1999, I was overcome by a burning desire to collect quartz crystals and experience their metaphysical properties.

Annie and I meet in junior college. I'd had a crush on her that was unrequited for 30 years. After missing my High School Reunion cocktail party by a week I came back to my sisters all dressed up with no place to go. I talked her into getting up; it was 10:00 Pm, and join me for a glass of wine. While at "Toots Lagoon" in Carmel, California. I heard the only other woman in the place laugh and found Annie.

Life was good now; I didn't have any serious expectations. I was living from one paycheck to the next like most of the still-working Americans. I'd see my sons occasionally and was looking forward to retirement and grand children.

So what was this all about? What was rocking my otherwise peaceful world? Suddenly obsessed with collecting quartz crystals, but with limited space, I had to rent a storage unit to make room for them all! I would have loved to keep them all around me, learning from each of these perfect expressions of Mother Earth. But I just didn't have room to display them all on the boat at one time. Instead, I'd get to know each one individually, then place it in a box to be returned to my storage on land.

I found most of my collection on the Internet. EBay was remarkably strong back in 2003. The old-find Lemurians were still available, some weighing over ten pounds. I don't know why I was so drawn to these beauties -- the rarity of them, I suppose.

Lemurian seed crystals were found in a layer of sand and clay, under a mountain that was being water-blasted in a strip-mining operation in Brazil.

Quartz crystals are found in what are called "vugs", small caverns where the hot silicon dioxide and water created the crystals long ago. No one knows how long ago that may have been, but it is known that it takes millions of years for erosion of the rock surfaces to expose them naturally.

The so-called Lemurian Seed Crystals were rare and unusual. It is said that they were stacked like cordwood, with one row lying on top of the next row. Quartz crystals grow in clusters, from one central point.

The Diamantina mine crystals, for instance, are water clear, with no horizontal striations, matte finish, or pink hue. They are particularly active with humans and will cause one to "tingle" from the hand that first touches it all the way up the arm to the pineal gland in the center of the head.

I found myself spending a lot of time researching all forms of quartz crystals. My crystal skull collecting began when I saw them on the Internet for sale. Then, somehow related to my passion for crystals.

I was then urged to visit my sister Stephanie in Carmel, California. As soon as I arrived, we visited an international import store with an eclectic assortment of treasures from around the world. I was especially drawn by all the quartz crystals, sparkling in the sunlight as I walked by the window. I could never afford the exotic treasures in the store, but the energy inside was palpable.

As I browsed browsing in the back recesses of the store, a flash of light caught my eye. I looked up with some surprise to see a gleaming quartz crystal skull. I don't know where the light had come from - perhaps it was a reflection from house lighting -- but it caught me and held me as if I were in a trance. It rested upon a high shelf in the back.

What I knew about skulls had to do with Halloween, witches, and black cats as do most uninformed people do.

I respected the excellent workmanship, and the price tag, and then moved on. Later that night while asleep at my sister Stephanie's, I had a dream, or perhaps it was a vision, that would plague me for the next two years. Now I question whether it was a dream or a vision. I don't know what it was.

"Way beyond your budget range! Don't blow your only retirement savings!" was my sister's impassioned response after I brought her to the back of the store and showed her the skull. I held my tongue; she would never understand, as her life was a struggle now with weighty responsibilities that she bore alone.

Stephanie is an extraordinarily tough and savvy woman who shoulders her burdens without complaint. However, she had no sympathy for what she felt would be a frivolous expenditure, especially at that difficult time. She could not know of the kinship I felt with all the crystals I had displayed around my boat. They were more beautiful to me than jewels. From the moment I would find one then having to bid at the last tenth of a second on eBay, a close relationship would begin if I won the bid. Each had its own story to tell, about how I came to possess it and where it had come from.

Then, as suddenly as it had begun, my crystal collecting ended. Most of my collection was in storage now. I had no more room on the boat! Increasingly, I felt the urge to display them, so I could see my collection in one place. Just as pressing, however, I wanted to learn to work with them, doing something worthy for mankind. And all the while, I had no idea why I was so obsessed with them, other than that it was a learning experience and was changing me on a deep level.

By 2009, the Great Recession was on and there was no work, so I had more time to myself. I mentally wrestled with hundreds of quartz crystals and minerals. I would move them back and forth, from storage to my boat and then back again into storage, spending time meditating with each one which at the time was new to me. I didn't have any long-range plan for them; they simply became a large part of  our lives.

I was mobile now after having both knees replaced due to a construction injury and arthritis. With time on my hands, I decided to visit my sons in the Seattle/Washington area. Along the way, I stopped in Monterey to pick up Stephanie. My sister happens to be a marvelous person to take on a road trip. She can drive and take care of all the details, as well as find excellent deals on accommodations and restaurants.

6

I neglected to revisit the Crystal Skull while passing through the Monterey Peninsula. I didn't want to face it, for there was no way I would spend a significant portion of my retirement on a Crystal Skull when I already had hundreds of specimens of all kinds of quartz and minerals. Thanks to Stephanie and Annie, I was "singing their song of "why spend so much when you have so many crystals now."

Stephanie happened to mention a mutual friend, a fisherman I worked with and later hired to work for me when I eventually ran my own commercial fishing operation. John Swinnerton is his name. He and I faced the worst weather, fishing winter crab and summer salmon and herring fisheries back in the early '70s. I had not seen or heard from him after the Exxon Valdez oil spill had wiped us out, twenty years before, and we, like most Alaskan fishermen, lost everything.

Little did I know he was living in Ashland, Oregon, that was right along the way when we were driving to Seattle, Washington. I called, and found him just by chance. He said he was looking forward to seeing us, and knew Stephanie from the old days when we lived in Homer, Alaska.

The trip to Seattle was wonderful; we split expenses and had an enjoyable experience traveling up the coast we stopping in Northern California to see Mount Shasta something about that mountain genuinely touches me. I am mesmerized by its grandeur. I had seen many mountains like it in Alaska over the past twenty years, but standing there, so regal and alone, with its snowcap, it is somehow magical.

We met John at a sidewalk restaurant in Ashland and spent the day visiting with him. Seeing his "Light Connector" invention was a treat. I tried it at his studio later on. Anyway, we bid farewell to John and headed up Interstate 5 to Seattle.

The skull dreams were especially vivid now as we neared Mt. Shasta. I had the same feeling I used to experience when I started collecting crystals, kind of butterflies in my stomach and a buzzing in my head.

We visited my sons, whom I hold respect and love for. My older son lives in a fine home on the banks of Lake Washington; visiting my younger son meant that we had to take the ferry to one of the islands in Puget Sound. Both were happy to see me and Stephanie again. The visit was way too

short, especially after we'd come
so far. However, seeing my boys
again was well worth it as
otherwise it would probably not
have happened for quite some time.

We then headed back, as
Stephanie had to return to work.
Once again we stopped at the city
of Mt. Shasta and drove up the
mountain as far as they would let
us. Melt-water was rushing from a
spring in a downtown park, so we
availed ourselves of some to take
home with us. What a grand place
to visit! This park had a magical
feeling, as if the "Wee Folk"
would be enjoying it when we
humans were out of sight.

Nevertheless, all the while,
I couldn't get my mind off the
blazing-eye dreams. Now they were
in my waking consciousness and I
was being tormented. It seemed
that somehow, as the vision became
more intense, the dreams and the
mountain had something in common.
I didn't have a clue as to what
that could be.

I felt at times as if I were
a little kid being pulled along in
a wagon by some Cosmic Big Brother
or Sister, and I was just along
for the ride, unaware of the
bigger picture. I supposed it
would all come out in the end.
Could this be what faith is all
about? Holding on to the sides of

your wagon and trusting fate will take care of you and has a purpose for this trip? This was new to a pragmatic ex-fisherman that always knew the tides.

Leaving Stephanie in Monterey I drove home, hoping for some work and looking forward to seeing Annie, my partner and best friend. Purposefully avoiding the import store, and the crystal skull inside it, I drove straight home.

I had a gnawing feeling in my gut, a queasy feeling like looking over the edge of a cliff, a kind of vertigo, when I thought about going to the import store. I feel now that I was fighting fate, and not acknowledging the destiny in store for me. It was a very disappointing and unsettling feeling for me.

GLOWING EYES


Chapter 2

During this time, I went online and told other crystal collectors I had met about my experience. All of these collectors wanted pictures of the skull that was inspiring my lamentations to them concerning my indecision.

I called the import store and asked the merchant if the Crystal Skull was still there. That was an interesting feeling after all I had been through in my dreams to be sure.

With mixed emotions about the unsettling thought of someone else taking the Crystal Skull home. It seemed as if I was waiting for some kind of sign to help me make a decision. I asked him to send me a couple of photos in an email.

"I remember you!" he enthused. "The skull -- yes, it's here, and it's waiting for you."" While acknowledging his words, I also tried to brush them off, knowing he was a high-end salesman who knew how to "hook" his intended customer. He declined to photograph the skull and send a few email-attached photos, as he said he was not proficient on the computer.

I called my sister Stephanie, asking whether she could drop in when in town and take a picture or two of the skull for me. She was up in arms right away! "YOU ARE NOT THINKING OF BUYING THAT SKULL, ARE YOU?" I assured her it was only curiosity, and a desire to show it to friends.

When I got the photos attached to her email, I was almost breathless. I was not ready for the seemingly monumental moment of looking at the first photo. She'd had the owner of the shop take the skull down from its shelf in the back and place it on his desk so she could take her photos.

The picture she sent was exactly like what I had been seeing in my dreams over the past two years. **(Fig.1)**

"Its left eye caught the flash of the camera, and it's this that has been haunting me all this time," I said out loud showing the picture to Annie. There was only one thing to do. This was the sign I had been looking for. As a fisherman, I'd learned to trust and follow my instincts. Having faith in what I was doing was the expression of what my subconscious already knew. I found myself hyperventilating. Having just returned from my trip to Seattle, it looked like I'd have to drive all the way back some four hundred miles to Carmel. I had to see this Crystal Skull again, as I now knew it was the glowing eyes haunting me.

I had to face it, along with the prospect of bringing this masterpiece of workmanship home. Flying up the 101 freeway, I was as giddy as a schoolgirl. This dear old friend, whom I had kept waiting far too long, had been calling me. No longer was it about the money. Could it be that this was tied into the epiphany I'd had about collecting quartz crystals? Once again I saw myself in the little red wagon.

My partner Annie was just as adamantly opposed to this large expense as was my sister; they were looking out for my best interests, I know. We all knew that I already had a world-class collection of rare Lemurian seed crystals, and nowhere to put them. How could I bring home another that cost so much?

"It's your money, and I know it's been calling to you for some time now, so go ahead and face it. But be objective, and don't let the salesman push you into something you'll later regret," she said, shaking her head as I drove off.

The import store looks deceptively small, considering the treasures inside. As I walked in, the merchant smiled at me, and said that my sister had been in to photograph the Crystal Skull.

"I would never take it down for anyone else, and I've had two other people looking at it. I'd not move it at all if I didn't know Stephanie as a local." I discovered that its back had what appeared to be a rock wall one inch "encapsulated" within the cranium, in solid, clear quartz. This was another stunning surprise for me. Handling the skull, I could feel the smoothness at the top of the cranium. I felt the converging lines of the different layers of quartz. There were three visible lines where one followed the joining layer. I could feel them with my thumbnail on the surface.

I was suddenly aware that this was an extremely fragile piece of quartz. I've had some of my collection fracture on a line like this with the least bumping or dropping. They say never to expose layered quartz to radical temperature changes, as it will not expand or contract evenly, and thus fracture.

This did not make any sense, as the colored matrix was totally encapsulated within one inch of pure, water-clear quartz. I felt the skull surface. The parent crystal it grew from became part of further layering twice more as it grew over millennia. When I turned it around to look directly at the back, it was a solid mass but, when viewed at an angle; it seemed so thin it all but disappeared. **(Fig.2)**

I was feeling a bit uneasy in my stomach; my head was pulsing with the sensation of a bright halo of light that radiated outward. I don't know how else to describe it, but maybe it was just a feeling of warmth that gave that impression. I knew I was definitely feeling something very different.

Sitting on a chair facing the owner's desk with shoppers all around me, I was self-conscious. However, I felt inclined to pick up the skull and press its forehead to mine! I had read that this is how shamans make contact with sacred skulls during ceremonies. I hadn't a clue what to expect, and had to overcome my self-consciousness in knowing I was being stared at. There were people all around, and I could feel some of the shoppers standing behind me and watching what I was doing. When I lifted the skull off its jaw, the merchant's face went white and he raised his hands but said nothing. I pressed the cool quartz to my forehead; it was so cold to the touch, but still I felt some warmth inside my head.

"OK?" the merchant said, looking skyward. He got up and left, evidently embarrassed as I continued to hold the skull to my head.

I was tingling, perhaps from the excitement of this long put-off meeting. But as I forced myself to close my eyes, I immediately got a vision of cave paintings. I had seen similar ancient paintings on the History Channel. The best way I can describe what I saw is stick men, painted on a rock wall. It was as if I were in a particular cave, witnessing these ancient drawings. The vision changed, and the stick men were in a three-part triangular grouping.

I was tingling and vibrating all over. I had a sense of peace, as if reuniting with an old friend from my previous dream or vision. Strange indeed! I also realized that I had stopped breathing, and had to take a giant breath, drawing even more attention to myself. Nearly overcome with self-consciousness yet I wanted to stay and see what else there might be for me to experience.

I placed the skull carefully back on its jaw. By now the Crystal Skull was wet from my hands, making it very hard to hold. The back was where all the weight was; it looked even, but this was an illusion. The main thing was that I had found what I was hoping for -- some means of communication with this quartz Crystal Skull. With my other crystals, I had the tingling sensation running up my arm and stopping in the middle of my head, but never any visions.

Further studying the beautiful patterned panorama on the back of the skull, again I felt that this was more than just a beautifully carved sculpture of rock quartz. How could the carver studying a large piece of quartz be able to see where the carving would let him align the rock matrix right in the center of the skull? Could it have been just a coincidence?

Perhaps it had something to do with the matrix itself. I had an interesting thought: It could be an ancient "memory bank" of information that, stored in the quartz, possibly wanted a way to get out. Whether through me or through someone else, the right person could awaken this long-sleeping entity.

It seemed to be hematite or iron oxide, which I was familiar with from collecting crystals, and was common. It was magnetic! This made me wonder if the slight electrical charge created by the iron could be stored in, or otherwise energize, the quartz crystal. My flight of fantasy was taking me nowhere. I somehow had to ground myself to deal with the reality of the situation.

I was drawing an ever-growing crowd of curious passersby, and the merchant was directing them away from me. It was then that I realized I was at an extremely critical junction in my life. I had an immense decision to make and had to be selfish with my time. I would disregard the probing feelings I was getting as the hair stood up on the back of my neck.

I just pretended I had a glass dome over me, and was cut off from the rest of the store. The only one I would let "in" was the merchant who, flitting around like a butterfly now, was torn between his new customers and some crazy-eyed person, handling his valuable Crystal Skull.

What would I do? Take a chance and buy it, and see where it would take me, or be conservative and just walk away? Take the safe way out from this new and magical experience that I could talk about, but never truly understand? This was the moment!

Now bringing it closer, eye-to-eye, I could see sadness in the eyes as the brows seemed to be angled downward toward the outside of the skull. Gazing deeply into those sad eyes, I searched for a sign that it would be all right. Nothing.

One eye served as a window into the skull. The other was a maze of foils and angles that reflected light back out at me. It was as if I were being drawn through its left eye into the large, clear area between the front of the skull and the layer of rock in the back. I couldn't allow myself to entertain this powerful sensation as over powering feelings I was receiving was bringing me to tears. Being in a public place and feeling the pressure of the merchant now crept into my consciousness as I felt his anguish wondering whether I was just sightseeing or seriously considering a large purchase.

The vision of the stick men was all I received. However, it showed me that we had a connection. It had chosen me as its caretaker and guardian. I'd been a commercial fisherman in Alaska for twenty years, facing many challenges that called for cool-headed fast-thinking, but none of that experience helped me in this present conundrum. I am usually pragmatic and can see through the usual smokescreens in life, but in special circumstances, I am called to disregard all else and follow my instincts alone.

This was something entirely new to me; I felt that I was way out of my league. Throwing caution to the winds, I decided to trust my instincts and purchase the Crystal Skull. This beautiful skull might be part of something more complex than I could presently understand. I felt it seemed to want to connect with me. The whole experience was seemingly way beyond my experience.

My instincts were to protect it as a possibly sacred, historical sculpture with some esoteric purpose. I would just have to wait and see whether my stewardship would bring me to a safe harbor. This is what my instincts told me. I had no other plan.

The merchant and I struck a deal after some haggling and agreeing not to divulge what I paid for the skull to anyone. He said he would not have come down in price but for the fact that he felt I would cherish the Crystal Skull and care for it, as his dear departed friend would have wanted.

I asked about the history of the skull -- where it was carved and when -- information called the "provenance."

"From the moment I saw you looking at it, I knew it was going home with you," he said. "The skull had been in a warehouse in Africa for twenty-two years. After the owner's death, his family, still living in Africa, liquidated the estate. His father brought the Crystal Skull into a more suitable environment, we bought it, and he then returned to Africa.

"We had it in the backroom for six years and only on display for the past two years. We put it out after the Indiana Jones movie." He looked down pensively. "It had been a memory piece for us to remember our beloved friend by. That's all I know," he said.

"We, my partner and I, agreed to sell it to someone we thought could feel the heightened energy it seems to put into a room," he said with a smile.

"If you bought it, then you must have the address of the former owner's parents still living in Africa," I put in hopefully, searching for an opportunity to investigate this family further. Shrugging, he smiled at me, declining to come forward with an address. I guessed that he had agreed to keep it a family secret. Now that the merchant had my money, he had no incentive to divulge any information concerning his friend or the history of the Crystal Skull.

He said he felt it had come from Idar-Oberstein, Germany, as his buyer had passed through there on occasion.

"They were said to have carved their skulls in the mid-19th century!" I blurted out. He had nothing further to say. There are no records of any carvers or sales of crystal skulls at that time.

So be it. All I knew for sure is that the person selling this particular Crystal Skull returned to Africa, his home.

I was giddy from this huge event, and just wanted to be alone with my fantastic find. I felt if there was more information, it would come out eventually. He wrapped it up in foam and placed

it in a cardboard box. I walked
out like a new father, careful not
to drop my precious bundle. I had
no clue how old my newborn might
be, but knew it was irreplaceable.

I felt there was so much
responsibility for me, with
everything hinging on blind faith.
I have taken many a chance
commercial fishing, but I always
felt that I had some measure of
control when it came to the
decision-making. Now, I was
casting my fate to what limited
information I had gleaned from
researching the legends of the
crystal skulls. This was an action
totally based on faith and the
image I received when holding the
skull to my forehead. The visions
I received convinced me there was
information that could be accessed
in a sculpture of a crystal skull.

At this time I knew nothing of
the abilities of crystal skulls
other than they were made of
Silicone Dioxide and therefore,
had the potential to hold
information as did the crystals in
my personal collection. It was a
matter of finding the means to
access this information.

All quartz is ancient, it takes
millions of years of erosion to
bring them to the surface for our
finding. So, carving a piece of
quartz into a skull would

logically be a signal there could possibly be information withheld inside. Other wise why not use an elbow or foot I was thinking.

STICK MEN

Chapter 3

I did feel contentment, driving
back to my sister's - a definitely
happy feeling, one of settling and
calming me. I was not thinking of
money at all. Driving with the
extreme caution of a new father
returning from the hospital, I
don't think I have ever driven so
slowly. Rationalizing the large
purchase, I thought about how this
artifact was unique and would
likely change my life in ways I
could not yet imagine. Still. It
was fun to fantasize. I remembered
hearing, "When one door closes,
another opens." It was up to me to
walk through it or not.

The hardships of my past --
the fall from operating a
successful Alaskan fishery and
living comfortably with my
beautiful family to suddenly be
all but destitute and having to
stay with my sister -- were
lessons in humility for me. Those
lessons continue as I discover how
ego is so undermining to the
positive energy of mankind.

I had lost everything, and all
because of one admitted alcoholic
in charge of one of the world's
largest oil tankers. I wondered

how many other stories of loss were out there among the 33,000 oil spill plaintiffs.

Upon reaching Stephanie's house, I could sense that she was all puffed up. I left the Crystal Skull in the car, not wishing to upset her and incur her further wrath, as I was spending the night and wanted peace.

"You bought it, didn't you? Didn't you? You look at peace with yourself. Might as well bring it in," she said off-handedly, as she turned on her heel and walked into the house.

I was happy that I was free now to inspect it more closely, and excited to tell someone about my experience. I carefully unwrapped it on the kitchen table. I was so worried about dropping it, especially breaking its jaw!

"Well, I guess it's your money," she said. "So what are you going to do with it?" I was speechless. I didn't know how I could justify this large purchase; I had no frame of reference and was still rather numb from the whole experience. I suppose I expected it to start singing or talking or something! I didn't have a plan so I ignored her question. Stephanie then placed a soft cloth on the table to set it on, and we just looked and gently turned it round and round.

The only crystal skull I had ever seen like this was photos of the famous Mitchell-Hedges Skull. It was found in 1924 in the Yucatan in an ancient ruin called Lubaantun. I knew that people lined up to see this crystal skull, so I figured these skulls must have something in them that made them exceptional.

One can see that the workmanship involved in carving a skull out of clear, natural crystal would take a master. Only a master could look at a piece of quartz and see and liberate a skull within it.

Now that I had the Crystal Skull, my collection was indeed world-class, and I felt that my future would work itself out.

After my Internet friends learned about the Crystal Skull, I started getting an education in the true purpose of the crystal skulls. These discussions centered on just why they are coming into human awareness at this juncture in our time on Earth.

There was much controversy swirling around the Mitchell-Hedges Skull, as some believed it was a prophetic find while others just figured that F. A. Mitchell-Hedges wanted some publicity and the assurance of future income for his daughter Anna.

The more closely I examining my Crystal Skull, it struck me that I had never noticed the rock matrix in its back area, nor the fact that the jaw was removable. At the import store, I had somehow missed these important features altogether. Were these good things, or had I made a mistake?

With no frame of reference, it was like being lost at sea in a life raft with this thing. Have you ever pulled out of a parking lot and not known where you were going, or which way to turn? That's exactly how I felt. I'd just have to have faith that the skull itself would somehow guide me. Now that I had made the huge commitment there was no turning back.

As I continued to admire the skull, *fantastic!* Is all that came to mind. How could the carver working with a large piece of quartz have revealed this rock matrix so perfectly in the center of a carved crystal skull?

The best way I can describe what happened is that it must have been like an intuition, when you instinctively know that something is hidden, and suddenly you find it right before you. It must truly have been a work of love.

I considered placing the
Crystal Skull outside overnight.
It was August 6, 2009, with a full
moon and partial lunar eclipse.
This skull had been in storage for
so long, and before that in a dark
warehouse that I figured it needed
to be "recharged" by the moon.
This was to be just the
beginning of the insights I would
receive from being around the
Crystal Skull. I placed her on a
table in my sister's dining room
with the moonlight streaming in.
My first impulse had been to place
the skull outside, but
my sister warned that there were
animals out there at night, and
was afraid they might damage the
skull, or that someone might steal
it.
Interesting, eh? From being
so totally against the purchase,
my sister had warmed right up to
the Crystal Skull and was now
showing considerable concern about
its welfare!
I was happy to see Stephanie's
nurturing. Was the Crystal Skull
also reaching her? I agreed to
keep it on the dining room table
where it would get the moonlight
all night and be safe. I got up
and checked it twice that night as
if I were on an "Anchor Watch" on
the boat. I had to admit that it
did have some capacity to ease the

atmosphere in a room. I would have to get more sensitive to this feeling.

From that night on, my dreams of the blazing eyes stopped. I also had a strong feeling that it was a female skull. The size was small for a man but still life-size and in portion.

The detachable jaw was a mystery; it looked so very fragile! This was the first time I had ever gambled so much on something I didn't feel I had control of. I'd thought nothing of spending this amount on fishing equipment or a new boat because I knew it was ultimately I who controlled the outcome. I could be almost certain of a good result by being committed to rising early and staying late, and by fishing aggressively, as I had learned from my past skippers. How wrong I was concerning this Crystal Skull! One simply did not push her.

I accepted that the outcome was out of my hands. I felt I was getting too old to go very far out on a limb. Still in my old fisherman mentality on a limb is where I had lived most of my life, having to fight for what I had and therefore being very competitive.

The day after coming home I Found, while surfing the Web on crystal skulls, a World

Mysteries Crystal Skull Conference, in Tempe, Arizona. Now was that was a coincidence?

Still overwhelmed by my commitment to this fabulous skull, I felt I had to continue the "run" and go be a part of something that I was being rapidly drawn into. Surely, the other skull caretakers would want to admire this magnificent sculpture and welcome me with open arms.

Annie and I sat with the Crystal Skull, visually memorizing every aspect. I bought a turntable, so we could see all sides without having to handle it. Rotating it – even on a smooth surface -- caused its teeth to slide and risk chipping.

The first impressions I received from her were as follows; She did not like to be handled, nor to be held or picked up, possibly due to her jaw, and she definitely didn't want to be underwater. I guessed these were associated with bad experiences in her past.

When I brought it home, I cleared the Crystal Skull as I learned to with all quartz crystal. As I was submerging her in a pail of saltwater, Annie freaked out.

"Don't put her underwater!" she shouted.

"Why not?" I asked as I reached in and pulled it out.

"The water might get between the layers and cause her to split apart!"

"OK, I'll just pour the water over her." Boy, Annie had sure come alive with the arrival of new Crystal Skull. Like my sister, she too had been against this major purchase. Now we were like new parents with a baby we weren't sure how to handle and care for.

We must have been funny to watch. Actually, we were getting some strange looks from the boaters around us, as I was always setting some crystals out on full-moon nights, and building crystal grids on the boat.

Annie had a more spiritual background than I, so I just followed along, smiling to myself as I did with Stephanie, relieved that I wouldn't be hearing about what a fool I was for bringing home a quartz crystal sculpture with nowhere to put it!

The Crystal Skull seems to be especially close to women; its feminine size and delicacy may have something to do with that.

Looking into its eyes, we both noticed what appeared to be a sad expression. I felt that he or she or it might have seen many terrible things, and that this may have been what the sculptor wanted to show.

We decided to call it a "she," as that was how she made us feel. Annie had already felt a female presence and a conviction that she would outlive us all. Giving her a name was not the issue, but rather determining what "she" represented to us. However, Annie and I felt it could be androgynous.

Her very being, and her name, therefore, could only be COMPASSION. Annie noted that compassion was everything she was -- sad yet nurturing, with unconditional love radiating from her silent but understanding eyes. The name came to us both as a simple matter of fact.

We both felt this warm radiation coming from her. Reaching this agreement brought a feeling that caused us to hold each other tightly. We felt the unconditional love all around us, filling the room.

This is when I decided to go to Tempe, Arizona, and see the other caretakers. I couldn't afford it, but felt I needed to get Compassion in the company of some "certified" ancient skulls. Because she is among the most beautiful of the crystal skull sculptures, anatomically correct and with a human-size movable jaw, and the most intriguing rock matrix in the back of her skull, I knew she would be well received.

I was certain that my fellow caretakers would have additional information about her, and that other crystal skulls like Compassion would be there. Bill Homann owned the only crystal skull I could find like Compassion. He lived with and cared for Anna Mitchell-Hedges for thirty years until her death. The M-H skull is totally clear; Compassion has the rock matrix in the back. Their jaws are somewhat different in attachment, as are number of teeth, but they're close to the same size and weight.

The anticipation of going to Tempe after only one month of adopting the new crystal skull, now called "Compassion," was consuming all my waking time, and I was having dreams of being with other caretakers, perhaps displaying our skulls on a grid. I could see us performing a ceremony for the good of mankind, which is what the skulls are said to be here for.

I had grown particularly close to this dear artifact. Over a relatively short period of time, a bond had been forming, similar to the kind I felt with an animate

being. She was no longer just an
unusual sculpture of quartz
crystal carved into a human-
looking skull; she was part of our
family. We often referred to her
for her insights and opinions out
loud. I never really got any
answer's however, Annie would
suddenly come up with things I had
never thought of. Like; don't
leave her in the Sun to long as
this will shatter the layering, Do
not placed her in water as it
might seep into the fractures
between the layering and cause
them to separate, etc.

I obliged sensing she had a
closer connection "as a female"
than I did. This was to prove to
be the case as women are more open
to there feelings than most men in
my humble opinion.

ATLANTIS

Chapter 4

Annie and I left on September 7th and met with 109°F weather, even before we left California with no air conditioning in my car. I had found a place that sells quartz crystals called Quartzsite, Arizona. They have a well-known yacht club. Funny, as they are over four hundred miles from any ocean.

We decided to stay there. It was 112°F, and we were very uncomfortable. The yacht club office was closed so we went to a local Mexican restaurant with some air conditioning to get a cold beer and wait. They said the yacht club would open at 5:00 P.M.

Quartzsite is like a ghost town, with boarded-up windows and sagebrush tumbling down the street. Signs blowing in the wind advertised Quartz for Sale, and RV Parking. We learned that in February, the town boasts one million residents, almost all of them snowbirds.. Now it barely seemed to harbor one thousand!

We soon noticed that, like the lizards, the locals went inside during the heat of the day; they started coming out as the sun

dropped lower in the Western sky.
I had to remember what I had
learned about true desert, and
that was respect! Finally, the
place opened up, and we went to
get a room. Turns out the rooms
are double-wide trailers.
Amenities included old-style swamp
coolers roaring away in the
stuffed window, their cold air
blowing directly onto the bed.

We agreed we needed to go to
the bar and get ready for a night
in Quartzsite; it would be a long
one. Having lived in the
Philippines for a year while in
the Navy, I was acquainted with
the humid and sticky conditions of
"wet heat." However, this was not
as uncomfortable. Dry heat does
sting, but I'll bet it's easier to
get used to.

The barmaid was friendly, and
I wound up buying a hat with the
Quartzsite Yacht Club logo
emblazoned on the front to show my
boating friends. After cold
drinks, delicious chicken, and
garlic pizza, we turned in. The
room was one of the most
uncomfortable I have ever stayed
in, and that includes other
countries. Somehow, we made it
through the night, and then got up
early to beat the heat and have
breakfast. We found a delightful
place and had a fantastic meal.

On the road again, Annie decided she wanted to go to Sedona, as it was only an additional one hundred fifty miles up the road. We were early for our event in Tempe, so we could swing through and see the place. Neither of us had been there in over thirty years. It was hot, but we were enthusiastic about the upcoming conference.

When we arrived, we were instantly lost in a maze of "European circles" controlling traffic flow. Round and round we went, trying to get to the downtown area. When we finally got there, we were in shock. My first impression was of a theme park in L.A.! To wit -- a strip mall, with water misting tourists from overhangs above the rustic-looking sidewalks. Gift shops with neon signs and the Honolulu Pink Jeeps! I suppose this should have been a sign for us.

After a while, we remembered that it's the people that make a place. The local people living a healthy and connected lifestyle were nowhere to be seen. As in Honolulu, the "locals" were outside the city limits.

We did locate a crystal shop, the only one in town we could find, and it was one of the finest I had ever been in. We hapened to find a large beanbag on which to rest Compassion atop her new turntable. The last time we were there, thirty years ago, there were mainly crystal stores and hippies; the atmosphere was authentic and hospitable.

We were silent as we left. The Buttes were as magnificent as before but seemed inaccessible without the Pink Jeep! The people I talked to later told me that the locals believe the energy had moved, due to the exploitation of the downtown area. The holistic energy had been replaced with "Made in China" trinkets.

Finding our way to the hotel was interesting. We got to Phoenix at about 9:00 P.M. After being almost killed by a Hummer pulling a Jet Ski so fast past the on ramp that the people in front of us simply stopped with no warning, we had to swerve onto the shoulder to avoid hitting a stopped, frightened driver. We then slid in the sand as we attempted to get back onto the road, finally managing to merge with some of the fastest drivers I have ever been around. I have no idea what happened to the cars behind me as they were pushing me to go faster to make the merge.

Gauging the unbelievable speed of oncoming traffic, and

then seeing the back of a car suddenly stopped right in front of us, had shaken me up! Adrenaline pumping, I'd immediately gone into survival mode.

"Why didn't you just stop? You didn't have to do a John Wayne around that car," Annie said, releasing her anxiety. We spent the next two hours arguing in the 109F heat about why I couldn't stop and how the car behind us had probably hit the car ahead of it. So, when we finally got to Phoenix, we had used up our patience and adrenaline, got lost, and were in extreme need of some air-conditioning. We were beyond speaking, and exhausted.

The Marriott Hotel lived up to the chain's reputation – air-conditioned and very elegant. Checking our bags in wet clothes from sweating in the car, it was still 109F at 9:00 P.M. We made our way to the room and unpacked. Following showers, we went downstairs to see if we could meet other caretakers.

Annie was so paranoid that she wanted to put Compassion in the hotel safe; afraid someone would come into our room while we were at dinner and steal her. I told her she needed a cold, stiff drink. After all, I reminded her, there had to be many crystal

skulls in residence, and all in
their rooms. We went to the bar to
drown our travel trauma and mend
fences between us. There we found
a couple of people drinking
...Pepsi!

I began to wonder whether
becoming a caretaker might mean a
change in lifestyle! I never
claimed to be a mystical person,
and didn't feel I had to act like
a purist or spiritual guy to be
caretaker of a crystal skull. We
had a drink and then dinner.

Was there a protocol I was
unaware of? We don't get out much.
The next morning we signed in and
got our name tags.
Annie's tag was among them; I was
intensely relieved I didn't have
to pay an additional $350 for a
second seat at the conference. The
scope of the place impressed us
greatly. We were extremely excited
at finally getting there after
almost 1,000 miles of driving,
including the trip to Sedona.

I'd hurriedly bought
Compassion an exceptionally cool
black foam-injected carrying case
just in time for our departure. It
was the finest I could find for
cameras and had a knob to regulate
the air pressure inside! Very hi-
tech!

"People sitting in the
audience will not be holding their

skulls in their hands, will they?" Annie asked. "You are not bringing Compassion in there, are you?"

"I am. I want people to see Compassion and I want to see other skulls." Online, I had asked the co-organizer for permission to introduce Compassion to the group and to get a table so I could show her. The answer was "NO!" I then asked whether I could introduce her, as she was so unique with her detachable jaw and rock matrix in the cranium. Again, it was a "NO!" Twice now so I dropped it as I didn't understand the protocols of a crystal skull conference and would just have to see for myself.

This conference was going to be crowded for me as I am 6'3" and three hundred pounds and take up some room. We placed Compassion on a separate chair between Annie and me. I knew Annie was somewhere between proud parenthood and self consciousness. She was sitting there holding the turntable level as the seats tilted back, afraid that Compassion's quartz jaw would slide off and fall onto the floor behind the chair. She was like a new mother -- out of character for her. I was proud she even came, much less accepted the responsibility of caring for Compassion.

The opening ceremony was particularly memorable and spiritual; we will never forget that ceremony. A man known as an Itzá Mayan daywalker, shaman, and elder performed it. His name is Hunbatz Men and says he is the spokesperson for the thirty Itzá Mayan tribes in Mexico. There were probably two hundred people there in the main room, with various merchants outside in the large anteroom. You could hear a pin drop when he spoke. Having never been in the presence of a Shaman I didn't know what to expect.

Being a large man I was cramped, and chose to sit in an aisle seat. When the ceremony was over, caretakers with skulls went up to the lectern to talk about the history of their skulls. I was hoping Bill Homann would be there so I could compare Compassion to his beautifully sculpted skull.

After the ceremony, I knew what I had to do with Compassion, for I was committed to being part of this new age of enlightenment that culminated with the Mayan Prophecy of 2012. Working for the good of mankind with this crystal skull was of course outside of my experience and comfort zone, but I accepted that it would be a process of growth. I would have to make the shift from personal wants and needs to those of my fellow men.

As Hunbatz Men walked past me, he glanced over at Compassion. He stopped and commanded me to "get up." Well, I am not used to being told to jump for anyone! However, I obliged and stood up in the aisle during someone's presentation. The shaman took his glasses from his briefcase and got down on his knees between the narrow seats to get an eye-to-eye look at Compassion.

Jennifer Welsh, who (I learned later) is well known in the world of crystal skulls, and a friend, were sitting right in front of us. They turned around in time to see Hunbatz Men point to the sky and say "ATLANTIS! This quartz came down from the Pleiades to Lemuria, and then to Atlantis, where it was carved!" The rock matrix in the back of the skull, and the fact that it was a true crystal sculpture with a moveable jaw, mesmerized him. He stood up, now saying for all to hear:

"This crystal skull came from Atlantis! The rock matrix in the back of the skull is a map, but I do not know where the map shows." He suddenly realized that his announcement had stopped the speaker. The whole audience was silent. He looked around to see one of the organizers, and then left abruptly. They had made some eye contact, perhaps conveying a message, and then he was gone.

We were totally ignorant at the time about the politics involved in these events. Evidently, the organizer had given Annie a complimentary pass to make it possible for us to attend, and encouraged us to make the effort. I felt Compassion is a significant skull, so many must have wanted to see her.    It seems that all this must have transpired prior to our arrival. But if they wanted Compassion to be there, why was I not allowed to introduce her to the others? It was especially frustrating to me that there was no place for attendees to showcase their skulls, so that they could interact with other caretakers who were walking around with their skulls in their hands, or sitting in the audience with them in their laps.

"Compassion, out of probably five hundred skulls, is the only human-size, clear quartz, and movable-jaw skull at this event!" Annie was saying to calm me down. Surely this was some kind of joke, especially given the convention-goers anticipation, and their keen interest in the history and purpose of the crystal skulls, as so movingly described by the spiritual leader, Hunbatz Men.

Just prior to the conference, I had read up on all of it, including the Singing Skulls.

The Mayan creation myth says that there were originally thirteen life-size human skulls of solid crystal and with movable jaws. The skulls were said to speak and even sing. The significance of the number thirteen is that the sun, the moon, and the ten planets in our solar system add up to the number 12. The last one signifies Quetzalcoatl, the serpent God, who will return to rule all the planets. The Mayan year was made up of 13 months of 20 days each. There are thirteen Mayan gods of the upper world. (From Angelfire.com, *The Mayans of Mexico*.
These skulls are also mentioned in the *Popol Vuh*.)

I was surprised that I hadn't seen a single one there, other than the one I brought. I'd expected to see at least a few. Moreover, because Compassion is unique due to her rock matrix, we would have had something noteworthy to share with all of them.

We were totally confused now. Was this "The Twilight Zone?" When

the known ancient crystal skull
caretakers were done taking turns
with their "interesting" stories
of how they came to be caretakers,
I noticed there were booths where
attendees could have their more
contemporary skulls "energized" by
the ancient skulls. The whole
thing had turned into an ordinary
gem and mineral show to me -- and
I have been to several!

Hunbatz Men had made it clear
that the purpose of the crystal
skulls was to teach us about a
different way to see things and to
live our lives. The ancients have
given them the energy and
intelligence to help us awaken to
the Shift in Consciousness that is
coming in 2012. (I didn't know at
the time this was the way they
were able to pay their expenses as
there travel and hotel was
provided by the host and all
proceeds of the door fee were kept
by the organizers).

Annie and I just wanted to
share Compassion with the
caretakers and those interested in
crystal skulls, we didn't have
anything to sell.

When ask by organizers if we
could have a table to show
Compassion and have an opportunity
to introduce her to the assembly
they said;

"What do you have to sell?" We looked at each other.

"Nothing, We just want to share our crystal skull Compassion."

While Annie and I were sitting in the audience, listening to the various speakers, I was trying to adjust to how things "really" were. Looking back now, I see I was getting my first "test" in the practice of higher thinking and living in Compassion and out of Ego...

I noticed then that the hair on the back of my neck had started to stand up. A man sitting by himself behind us about fifteen rows seemed to be concentrating on us, and pretty soon I could feel his energy in the hair on the back of my neck starting to "tingle." He had moved right behind us. He introduced himself as Gerald. I asked whether he was Bill Homann, the current caretaker of the Mitchell-Hedges Skull, as he looked like Homann.

"No, but I'm acquainted with the skull." He said he had been sitting back looking at the rays of energy coming off the crystal skull Compassion during the stories on stage.

As he stood there watching Compassion with his hands outstretched to feel her energy, his eyes started to moisten; tears were flowing down his cheeks as he explained this anomaly in a calm voice (as evidently he was used to explaining this).

"My eyes water when I am in the presence of a sacred object. I travel the world in search of these objects as I am directed to do by intuition." He said wiping his eyes. We talked for a while, and agreed to stay in touch to see where our paths would lead us. He thanked us for taking the expense and time to bring such a powerful skull to the conference; he said we would meet again.

At this point Jennifer, still sitting directly in front of us and having turned around to see Compassion, asked us about bringing her own personal skulls into the conference. I wondered who told her she couldn't.

"Sure! We want to share with other caretakers too," I said. She hurried out and brought in her two skulls and two large discs that were sacred artifacts of some kind. I was told they were used to amplify the energy of the skulls.

I was confused why the attendee's, especially some with such interesting skulls didn't feel it was appropriate to share their own skulls with other attendees. This was a large learning curve for us.

ATTENDEE ANARCHY

Chapter 5

I noticed a table toward the end of the first day of the conference. It had a tablecloth and was at the end of a long row of seats that was empty, at the stage end of the room. A fellow attendee was placing his three exceptionally beautiful skulls on the table. I walked over and asked him whether they were for sale.

"No, these are from my personal collection. I just wanted a table to show them to the others. I just got back from Peru, and am proud of my new collection," he said. Well, this was all the encouragement I needed. The Universe was speaking clearly.

The next morning, the second day of the conference, Annie placed our turntable in the center of the table, and we took up residence behind the otherwise empty table. Our little display attracted a good number of conferees that also wished to show off their skulls and share information. We'd followed the lead of the young man who felt as we did, and had the courage to take the initiative and create a place for all of the attendees to share their skulls. **(Fig.3)**

This skull conference surely could not have been ALL about just selling and sharing by a select few, could it? When I asked this young caretaker about it, he said he had found a place and obtained permission to display his personal collection of crystal skulls at the end of this unused table. Both were water-clear and beautiful. He'd flown in from Peru just in time for the event, and said he was not feeling well.

Thanks to the initiative this one man took, from that point on the event really took off for all the attendees. We started meeting people and sharing right away. Meeting with my fellow skull caretakers is what I'd come for.

"How could you have a crystal skull conference and not make it possible for the attendees to share?" I said to Annie.

"Compassion represents compassion, forgiveness, and unconditional love," Annie reminded me. "The energy of the skulls will bring us together."

We shared what we had heard about the legend of the 13 skulls, along with possible ramifications of December 21, 2012. This was the interest of those who soon gathered around what I called the "anarchy table."

What Hunbatz Men said was being reinforced, and that was the most crucial part of the event for me and the people gathered around the table. These people understood the Creation Myth, and some had heard of the movable jaw "Singing Skulls."

I was reminded of how much skull caretakers need to network with one another, and promote the spirit of the Mayan prophecy concerning 2012. Most understand the coming era to be about unconditional love for one's fellow man and the Earth. It's about moving away from the greed for power and profit that has wreaked untold environmental damage in the name of progress and dominance. Annie just looked at me and smiled.

We had an immediate crowd of people wanting to place their skulls in front of Compassion. They said they wanted them to be activated or energized.

Now I was seeing how it works. This was all so new to me; I was unprepared to have Compassion energize anything! Of course, we agreed as they started placing beautiful crystal skulls in front of Compassion's turntable. Some of the most beautiful skulls now

emerged from the protective bags
or hands they'd been carried
around in before there was a place
to share them.

In all the years I've worked
with crystals, I always had to
"touch" a crystal, which would act
as a conduit between the crystal
and me, or between two separate
ones. This is not the way I found
it to be with Compassion. About
eight inches from any part of her
cranium is powerful, and if you
take your palm, and once the
energy is felt, move it outward
from the skull the energy will
follow you.

While we were not selling
anything, we of course respected
the merchants, such as Leandro de
Souza, who were making a living
selling their carved skulls. We
were still assimilating the
powerful opening ceremony of
Hunbatz Men. I took to heart the
things he'd told us all, and still
believe them.

"It is our responsibility as
caretakers," he'd stressed. "We
are the New Maya; it is ours to
spread the word of the ancient
Maya to prepare for 2012."

In subsequent personal
correspondence he'd written: "I am
truly glad to hear from you and
Compassion again. I think all the
things you say, and of course your

new book, are particularly important. By the way, it is a great honor for me to have my name in your book. You have my consent to do that.

"I have written the *PROPHECY OF THE CRYSTAL SKULLS*. If you want to include this writing or part of it in your book, it is fine with me.

"The content of this writing is extremely sacred for me because it is part of the teachings transmitted to me by my uncle and teacher Don Beto, the last shaman of Espita, my hometown, where I was born long ago.

I don't have room for all of it; however, I feel it's essential to illustrate the point that according to the ancient Mayan creation myth, crystal skulls talked and even sang to the Maya' and were called, therefore, The Singing Skulls.

There should be a very fundamental reason why the modern humankind is getting eager, day after day, to know the true reason for the existence of these crystal skulls and their mission in this world. It has been known that there are some groups of scientists that are trying to know more about them, as well as groups of people who make meditations using the crystal skulls to make

contact with other dimensions
through them; many of these people
claim to have received messages
from these crystal skulls.

Below is what I have copied
from the original version of
*Hunbatz Men, Daywalker, Shaman,
and Spokesperson of the Itzá Maya*:

*"As a representative of the
Maya Tradition, I think it is
necessary to tell you what once my
Maya teacher and uncle,
Don Beto, taught me about the
crystal skulls. I remember some of
his wise teachings, as for
instance the following one.
Once we were sitting near a cenote
(eye of water) in Wenk'al,
watching its waters, when suddenly
my uncle stood up and stopped at
my back; he asked me to stare at
my face's reflection on the
water's surface for a while, and
he also told me that he would be
around watching me at a distance.*

*I obeyed his command and
looked at my face reflection in
the water for some time; due to
the solar light, I noticed that
the reflection of my face turned
from white to transparent at
times. There was a moment when I
started to have some fun because
of the different colors and shapes
my reflection experienced. It was
so funny to see how one of my ears
stretched out, or how one of my*

eyes seemed to disappear, but after some time, I felt as if I were entering an unknown dimension, and then I became a little frightened.

But the most shocking moment for me was when I saw another face reflecting next to mine on the surface of the water. My first thought was that it was the reflection of my uncle's face, but when I turned around to my left side, I could see my uncle Don Beto sitting down at an approximate distance of 15 meters from me; he had been waiting in the same spot all this time.

Even though I was so puzzled and scared, I looked back at the surface of the water and then I got a real surprised! My face had turned into a skull. The strangest thing is that right at that moment I began to feel so calm and relaxed. A few minutes later, I saw the skull turn into a transparent color and start to emanate a very bright light.

From time to time, I noticed that its jaw moved as if it were opening up, and through the basins of its eyes I began to see many pyramids.

It may be said that I began a trip through the skull's eyes, and I saw many things. Perhaps it was my own skull that had transported

*me to that wonderful trip. I am
not quite sure of it, but what I
can assure and affirm is that I
saw many things on that trip.
Someday I will write all the
experiences I had in a book. I was
still wandering in that dimension
when I suddenly felt some pats on
my back and heard a voice calling
me, 'Hunbatz! Hunbatz! Hunbatz!
Come back! Come back! Come back!'"*

Reading this, I am truly
honored to include this experience
of Hunbatz Men. I'm sure he made a
positive impression on every
caretaker present. I am trying to
live up to the responsibility of
suddenly becoming the caretaker of
a Sacred Crystal, Singing Skull.

Compassion is one of two such
skulls that I know of in the world
at this time. Men's response to
her was a possible affirmation of
Compassion being pre-Columbian.
The Maya said the "Star People"
came to them and brought the
crystal skull with them to teach
new ways, possibly using them as
computers in their time.

We were attracting quite a
crowd now in front of the table.
People were waiting their turn to
display their own skulls; some
left them and went off to shop,
trusting us to care for their
skulls.

Compassion always has a Lemurian Seed Crystal to keep her company. Sometimes I include four large ones I call the Sentinels; the Sentinels make me feel comfortable as they serve as a protective grid. Some have the same occlusion she has. I feel on a deep level that there has to be a strong connection between these crystals. At times when I am ask to present compassion to a group of people I bring along a series of four huge Lemurian Seed Crystals I refer to as the "Sentinels." I feel they form a grid around Compassion using the four cardinal points; North, South East, and West.

I do this out of intuition or instinct. I have no training Shamanic or any other discipline. It just seems right to create a type of Temple setting as I have the crystals and I feel Compassion is a Sacred Object.

Some have told me it's holding her center and grounding her. Others say it's for a protective grid so any negative or evil cannot enter her sacred space. I leave it up to the people that are willing to share their time with Compassion.

CAROLE DAVIS

Chapter 6

A particularly intriguing woman came up to us, Carole Davis, coauthor with Brian Hadley-James of *The Skull Speaks* and *Beyond the Veil of Time*.

The only person given private access to the Mitchell-Hedges Crystal Skull over a period of two years in the '80s, Carole engaged in the channeling of an entity through this skull. Carole was, and continues to be, accepted by the family of the Mitchell-Hedges caretaker.

*The Skull Speaks* was the first book of its kind on the power of the crystal skull found by British explorer Frederick Mitchell-Hedges. Printed in 1985, the limited edition sold out almost instantly, and became a collector's item. Now, in 2010, a rare copy is selling for quite bit. This lends credence to Carole's ability to channel the entity located inside the skull, or in this case what seems to me to be an extraterrestrial intelligence that is using the crystal skull as a resonating chamber for transmission to the medium.

Carole is well known and respected as someone who will tell the truth in all matters, including a crystal skull she does a reading on. This in itself seems to be an exceedingly rare commodity these days. A handsome and particularly well-educated young man, an old friend of the family accompanied Carole.

When the scheduled speaker didn't show up, Carole was asked to make an impromptu presentation to the group. She gave a brief account of her experiences with the Mitchell-Hedges Skull. Then she was asked by Jaime Maussan, a well-known journalist and ufologist who is the caretaker of the ancient crystal skull called "Rosie," to do a reading on his skull.

The carving date of a crystal skull cannot be verified, nor can its location of origin be found with any accuracy because it's a silicon-based object with no carbon to date. Further, it's not the age of the quartz itself but rather when it was actually carved. This information given in ancient ceremonies through high priest is said to be downloaded to these skulls. It would be difficult to verified as to exactly when a skull was carved I feel, except for contemporary skulls with photograph evidence.

Touching a skull, Carole can evidently determine if the skull is ancient or just another contemporary skull. Some skull wholesalers have gone to the extreme of "burning" raw sugar onto their recent skulls to make them appear to have been underground for thousands of years, and there doesn't seem to be any end in sight, as they are only doing what they feel they need to do to make sales. Who's to know when they were carved? In this case, location provides a clue, as Rosie was said to be dug up at an ancient site.

No individual skull to date has been specifically linked to the Mayan Prophecy or the myth of the 13 skulls! The focus seems to be on establishing if a particular skull is ancient, and therefore more valuable.

Carole can only speak the truth as it comes through her. She has no memory afterwards of what was revealed in deep trance. However, today she was just giving impressions as she handled the skull.

Carole has the sensitivity to get this information from crystal skulls, and is totally impartial. As a rule, I don't follow channeling, but after hearing

Hunbatz Men and the reading Carole gave Jaime Maussan concerning the exact spot where this skull was found, I felt she was authentic.

I gained a lot of respect for this woman that day; straightforward, she didn't make any excuses or pull any punches. I was understandably uneasy about Compassion coming from Atlantis, as Hunbatz Men had said as I had no background on him. I was not 100% sure that the legendary continent of Atlantis had even existed, as people were locating it everywhere from Central America to the Caribbean, the Bikini Atoll, and the Mediterranean, on Santorini Island.

I would be happy if everybody had agreed on just one place. I kind of felt the Caribbean was a logical place after reading anthropologist George Erikson and Professor Ivar Zapp's fascinating book, *Atlantis in America.*

Being a career mariner, I understood their work and considered their theory feasible, especially since the oceans of antiquity were as much as four hundred feet lower than they are today. The Minoan ruins uncovered at Santorini Island, and the subsequent story of Akrotiri, had somehow stirred my heartstrings. I suppose if Atlantis were very powerful, it had settlements in strategic areas on many coasts.

Sometime around closing time, Carole came to our table space. She spent time examining Compassion, revolving the turntable and running her hands over Compassion as if caressing a baby. This would normally cause me alarm, as I ask people to refrain from touching her for fear of damage to her fragile jaw and the likelihood of imprinting left on the quartz. However, I had no trepidation whatsoever, as I could see Carole was not trying to lift the heavy skull, but to feel its surface and its energy.

When she came to the rock matrix on the back of Compassion's head, she stopped. This was the same place where Hunbatz Men had stopped on the skull.

Carole immediately called for a piece of paper and a pen. She started drawing all kinds of figures and symbols. I was extremely excited to get this information. Offering her my seat, I could see that she was not in a trance, just telling us what she saw from the skull. She could barely keep up with the information she was getting,

We soon had a large crowd wanting to hear this reading, as

Compassion was only the second crystal skull Carole had ever read that gave her direct information, she told us later.

"The information is coming so fast that I cannot keep up!" Carole said. Annie instinctively took the tablet and pen and kept on writing and drawing the symbols Carole was observing.

"How does this information compare with the readings you did on the Mitchell-Hedges Skull?" I had to ask.

"With the Mitchell-Hedges Skull, the information was not moving. It was the same every day. I'd just go into meditation and let the entity talk through me. With Compassion, the information is coming from the skull itself, and at a very fast clip. It is downloading information at me in a Kaleidoscope with such a remarkable rate of speed that I can grab only bits and pieces."

After about thirty minutes, her escort lightly touched her arm, reminding her that they were soon to dine. Carole left saying she'd enjoyed the session and would like to see Compassion again when she had the time to become better acquainted with her.

"This is the only skull that actually spoke to me," she said over her shoulder as she was walked away. "The skull said to me, in a loud voice, WEE! WEE!' I can imagine her being happy to be out of the warehouse,'" Carole said. And with that, she disappeared into the crowd. It was the last time we saw her.

Annie was so excited to get some information from Compassion; this was the verification I felt we needed. For me personally it validated my final decision to bring Compassion home. I wondered if Annie too might be getting more information than she was sharing.

She holds her cards close to her vest, as they say. I would have to just wait and see what she came up with when we were together later on.

For the attendees this was their opportunity to see and experience the ancient crystal skulls they had heard about, and now a chance to share with their own stories. Possibly, they would take something meaningful back with them as a memento of the experience. I was just a newcomer trying to figure out the dynamics of the whole crystal skull conference agenda.

Excited and encouraged by what Hunbatz Men had acknowledged and what Carole Wilson had received, it was now clear to us that

Compassion had something important
to share. When she was carved no
longer seemed so important.
However, pragmatic soul that I am,
I felt I needed more proof.

I still wanted to ask Carole
so many questions, such as where
and when she'd been carved. Was it
in Atlantis? But it never came up.
It occurred to me that the
information it holds in the quartz
could be millions of years old,
and too complex to "sort out."
At this point I decided, *It's not
when a skull was carved -- it's
what it does!* What is it doing
today? Is it working for the good
of mankind as Hunbatz Men told us
the Mayans had taught?

I knew now in my heart that the
crystal skull Compassion is so
much more than a fine work of art.
She is an anatomically correct
human form that somehow holds
information that we are trying to
find a means of accessing. They
are here, all the skulls to teach
us something I feel. Some are
accessed by sound, i.e. toning
with the human voice or singing
bowls. Others could use different
lights while the observer focuses
on the skull. Learning to listen
seems to be the lesson with the
skulls.

I am not the one to give advice
as Compassion has only been with

me a short time. Other caretakers
with years or even decades have a
wealth of knowledge to pass on. We
just have to ask them.

Compassion speaks for herself,
this means I am not the conduit
only a chronicler of information I
receive so I try to keep my
personal experiences with her to
myself. I feel the strongest
evidence is the response to her on
an intuitive level of those that
have sat before her. However, with
a revealing book like this I have
to give my views to make a story.
It's a huge learning curve for
someone with no experience with
skulls much less a professional
writer so make up your own minds
on this.

LEANDRO de SOUZA

Chapter 7

A fellow introducing himself
as James Ziegler from Brazil made
his way through the crowd and
approached our little table. Owner
of "Stones of Brazil," he had
heard about this unusual crystal
skull and wanted to see
Compassion. Having imported the
largest number of carved crystal
skulls in the U.S., he is
considered an expert in his field.

James watched closely as I
turned the skull around for him.

"WOW! I have to get my friend
Leandro to see this!" he said, and
sped off through the crowd. Soon,
a soft-spoken gentleman was
standing before Compassion. Others
sensed something in him and moved
away. He kneeled down as if in
prayer and gently ran his fingers
over Compassion's nose and eyes,
caressing her like a lover; he was
experiencing her with the hands of
a master carver with closed eyes.

Leandro was so taken with
Compassion that it was palpable to
everybody watching; all were
silent as he got on his knees and
took measurements with his fingers
and knuckles to judge proportion.
All we heard from him was,

"Fantastic." This was said softly, as if he were speaking with her himself.

James told us that Leandro was the master skull carver in Brazil, and had been for twenty years. They conferred back and forth in Portuguese. I asked about the rock matrix in the skull and they agreed it was feldspar, and that the red was an iron-oxide occlusion. It had been encapsulated between the layers of Quartz when it cooled.

They both agreed it had not been carved in Brazil, nor had the quartz come from Brazil. This was a surprise to me, as I didn't know one could tell just by looking at the quartz where it had come from. They didn't even look surprised; it was just a matter of fact. They'd worked with tons of quartz from around the world but, of course, mostly from the most abundant source, Brazil.

I told them that the skull was found in Africa, and they agreed it might have been African quartz as they were not familiar with this particular variety.

"How can this be?" I said to Annie. "These men are the leaders in the industry. James has spent twenty years finding the quartz and organizing one of the largest warehouses in Brazil for crystals.

He probably produces more skulls of all kinds than any competitor, and Leandro is the master carver."

Leandro is an artist who actually sees with his hands. Like Michelangelo, who chipped away at blocks of marble to reveal the lovely figures that he saw within them, Leandro "finds the skull" within the quartz.

"Allowing the stone to tell me what it wants to be," he says he sometimes has to wait years before the crystal or mineral tells him where and how it wants the face to be carved.

Annie and I were elated to learn that Leandro de Souza is the foremost skull carver in the world. I asked him about the jaw being from the same quartz, and if it were cut from the skull.

He said that these days, cutting a jaw from a skull is all but impossible, as the vibration of the grinder would shatter the jaw -- the usual sad outcome when this is attempted. Sculptors do not even try anymore, he said, as their work is usually ruined, and it takes so long to carve a skull.

Compassion's jaw appeared to have been cut from the skull, but he could not say for sure. However, he believed it was from the same quartz as the skull. That conclusion they both did agree on.

I notice a pretty lady had been watching the proceedings, and after Leandro and James left to cover their crystal-skull resale table in the next room. Suddenly this "glowing" woman stepped up to meet us she had the most sparkling eyes, and her Irish brogue was authentic. She took Annie and me by surprise, as we were still buzzing about meeting James and Leandro.

Jane introduced herself and her business manager, Mort. He was a large man, someone you'd not want to pick a fight with, except that he had the kindest eyes and was hovering over Jane, almost as if he were her bodyguard. Jane is a world-renowned physic medium, a frequent guest on radio and TV programs.

"This skull is very powerful," she said. Without touching her, she placed her hands over Compassion, saying, "You have to clear all blockages and be very sure of your intentions." She looked me directly in the eyes and held them. "This crystal skull will boost your intentions ten times in the direction your heart tells her to. She goes and comes from your heart. She is ready to download information, and you better be ready for it."

She looked at Annie and me with a serious stare. She went on with what seemed like a warning.

"If your intentions are impure or selfish then the energy she pours through your Physic will fracture like a broken mirror and most likely damage you spiritually." She would not say what that intention had to be, but it seems to relate to my being chosen as caretaker of Compassion. This was my personal challenge from a very pretty, little Irish woman we just met! Annie understood right away.

"This crystal skull is still activating," she said. This bothered me, as I didn't have any intentions other than providing a forum for Compassion. I felt I was just the caretaker and guardian. I was no physic medium or even a metaphysically trained person.

Annie and I had spent so much time with Compassion that we came to the only conclusion, which is that she, Compassion, speaks for herself. It is my job as caretaker and guardian to bring her to people and keep her safe from harm.

I don't speak for Compassion. I try not to give my personal impressions of what Compassion has said as I have an obvious conflict of interest. (This was going to be another test coming up for me.)

Annie and I are committed to bringing Compassion to as many people as we can. It is up to them to take away from the experience what they will, just as we were doing now at this conference. I had to sit and think about what Jane had to say and consider opening myself up so that future communication with Compassion could be accomplished. This would require work on my part.

As I have said, I am not a trained metaphysical person; I don't go to workshops. I am much like most of the people I am talking to. I have the astrological sign of Cancer, so I live on the water and am happy to stay at home.

However, now I knew just where to start. As we were leaving, I found Jane and Mort. I asked whether she had time to do some work on me in the form of helping me clear the blockages she had alluded to. Then I would be better able to receive Compassion's downloads, Jane agreed. This session was more than I had anticipated and extremely productive. I usually abstain from this work, as there are so many people who, shall we say, have read all the books and been to all the workshops yet are not anchored in their own work.

It was a first for me, and just the beginning. I felt like Alice in Wonderland falling down the rabbit hole. From making the two-year decision to buy this crystal skull to overhauling my spiritual self to conform to her needs, it was an intense time for me. An hour after being brought back up from the session, I felt lighter and a little dizzy, with plenty to contemplate. This session was very painful and personal, one of the most profound experiences of my life. I shall never forget how much Jane dug inside and opened me up. Now she and Mort were off to Spain, as she had just spent five years doing a radio show in Dublin, Ireland. I will miss her and Mort.

It was now the 10th of September 2009. I had been with Compassion for a little over a month but already so much had happened. My life would never be the same. Through it all, I was so happy that Annie could accompany me, as she is my grounding "stone," and if ever I needed a rock, it was this day.

COMPASSION WITH ORBS

Chapter 8

Annie and I drove away from the first and most unforgettable conference we could imagine. With spray bottles showering us with cold water as we discussed what a major life-altering event it had been. I was helped by Annie to realize that the positives greatly outweighed any disillusionment I might have had.

I believe it was the people we met at our little space at the table who had made the event so very meaningful to us. None of the other caretakers of ancient skulls came by if nothing else but curiosity of the only crystal skull present with a movable jaw. However, they were busy at their booths. They have been doing this for years so this is how it's done.

It was a huge learning curve for me to welcome and integrate. Annie and I vowed to keep in touch with the wonderful people we met, and we are doing to this day.

"This is where you need to focus your energies," Annie reminded me. "Your personal intentions have to be reevaluated

for their deepest meaning.
Remember what Jane told you."
Over the years, Annie was to
repeat this to me, almost as a
mantra. Sometimes it felt as if
she had a big club to use every
time slipped into my usual mode of
thinking. When we returned home,
my partner reminded me: "It's all
about Compassion now." Looking
back now after two years, I can't
tell you how often I heard that
and repeated it to others.

This was to take some deep
meditation and ongoing spiritual
work, which became my focus upon
our arrival back home. However, I
am still a pragmatic fisherman at
heart.

"Compassion is very nice, but
she's not well enough known for us
to make it worth our while.
Sorry." This was the response, in
essence, when I called around to
see about showing Compassion at
metaphysical stores close to where
we live. I had never thought that
just seeing Compassion was enough;
one needed to feel her to know and
see she was a one-of-a-kind
sculpture – and presence -- in the
world.

Had I followed the popular
route and claimed she was found in
a temple or given to me by some
medicine man I could then claim
she was ancient and joined so

many. This was not in me. Telling
the truth as I know it to be and
thereby taking what I call the
high road is a lonely path.
Compassion is not famous for
anything other than with this
crystal skull has to offer and
what people's response has been.

I know now that I have chosen a
separate path from some well
mainstream crystal skulls. I can't
seem to get past thinking about
how the purpose of the crystal
skulls is the different from what
I was seeing at the conference. I
was reminded that all roads lead
ultimately to heaven. I needed to
move beyond this as I have learned
not it's Ego.

While I was in one particular
store, a woman who was doing
readings there suggested we
contact a woman she knew who held
special events at her home. She
said she would contact her, and
then she could contact me. I
agreed, and later met a most
delightful and enchanting woman.

I found Katherine Rosengren
living comfortably with her
husband and daughter. After we
became acquainted, Katherine had a
chance to experience the crystal
skull Compassion. She told me that
she was familiar with other
skulls. I told her that Compassion
would have been with me for one

month on the next full moon and asked if I could perform a Full Moon Celebration in her backyard. It was an ideal place for it as she had a sizable expanse of lawn. She said she would invite her friends who were open to this type of thinking and make it invitation.

Katherine's husband Harold is a successful doctor who did not have any experience with crystal skulls. Katherine assumed he'd have no interest at all. However, Harold sat down before Compassion, mesmerized, and spent the time we were meditating in her living room staring at Compassion. He said afterwards that he'd experienced an unusually warm feeling and felt at peace while looking deeper and deeper into the left side of Compassion's skull.

"It seems to go on forever," he remarked. Dreaming about the upcoming celebration, I had visions of a circle within a circle. I wanted to incorporate my large collection of crystals into a grid around Compassion.

I loved the way the dolphins on Compassion's new little pedestal were twined around each other, holding up a clamshell on their noses for her to rest on. It reminded me of something that might have been fashioned in

Atlantis out of marble. I placed my turntable on top of the clamshell, and Compassion on top of that. A round wicker end table on the grass worked well to stabilize the pedestal. I was very excited at the prospect of showing Compassion to people who would understand how unique she was and possibly gain some personal information.

Annie was concerned that the whole pedestal would fall over if someone accidently bumped into it. I assured her I would be there to do the turning of the turntable and that I was acutely aware of the stability issue. However, I wanted people to be able to look Compassion right in the eyes, and see what would result from experiencing the matrix inside the back of her skull.

I wanted a two-ring grid of Lemurian crystals. This would include nine large Lemurians pointing upward, on their own round teakwood bases, to create the outer perimeter of a circle. Thirteen smaller Lemurian crystals would lie horizontally around the base of the pedestal. I chose these numbers of Lemurian crystals totally at random; only thirteen would comfortably fit around the pedestal, and I had only nine ten-pound Lemurians mounted upright on teak bases.

The vision I had was of a gathering around Compassion, with the guests inside the outer perimeter to best receive the Sacred Feminine energy coming with the full moon. I kept hearing that Compassion is the living embodiment of the Sacred Feminine. I find these dynamics hard to articulate: they are relayed to me intuitively, with no words.

The energy would be coming in from the Moon, her moonbeams passing through Compassion and reflecting on the thirteen radiating crystals, then to the guests and then along the outer parameter of the anchoring vertical ring.

As the light radiates upward to the Universe, it also turns downward into the Earth, grounding that energy. I truly felt sending the unconditional love upward and downward, while becoming totally immersed in the incoming power of the "Sacred Feminine."

Katherine had some tiki torches in the yard, so I placed them along the perimeter of the outer circle. All of this conformed to the vision I'd had. Did it come from Compassion? Honestly, I don't know. I'd just more or less "day-dreamed" it. What a rewarding sight to see, especially with people gathered around, holding hands as the moonlight streamed through Compassion to the crystals.

A man contacted me a few days earlier who said he had shamanic training in Peru, Egypt, and Mexico. His name is Andrew. He had seen our flyer, and the fact that Compassion had been in a warehouse in Africa for twenty-two years. He wanted to bring his woman friend Jenny, who "tones" with her voice while he plays his shamanic drum.

Annie and I were honored to have them as guests, as this event was by invitation only. Katherine has many friends who share her metaphysical orientation. I told Andrew and the lovely Jenny about my configuration of crystals.

"How many of your Lemurian crystals are you using?" he wanted to know. I told him eight on the outside and thirteen around the pedestal, which makes twenty-one. Then I lit up saying, "With Compassion it makes twenty-two!" He gave me a knowing smile and shared the smile with Jenny. He said he knew he was at the right place now.

I ask people not to touch Compassion. A fellow caretaker had tried to pick her up at the Tempe Conference, as if she were like a discrete one-piece skull. Not only was he unaware of her removable jaw -- he also didn't realize how unbalanced she was, and came very close to dropping her on her jaw! This almost gave me a heart attack. Annie shot me a look that would have blistered paint!

"Never let anyone touch her again," Annie made me vow. I'd not be the one who let her get damaged after all the years she had been carefully stored or cared for. This was extremely serious. If the crystal skull gods didn't get me, Annie would for sure! As a woman, Annie was evidently closer to Compassion than I realized, as she would make knowing comments with no explanation.

The guests arrived. I was following "industry standards" by charging a gate fee to see Compassion. I learned this from the conference; I understood the purpose but could get past my feelings of the mass marketing atmosphere as I had seen in Gem and Mineral shows I had attended in my past when collecting crystals.

This money-charging made me feel decidedly uncomfortable, suspecting that Compassion was unhappy being used for personal gain, which of course is not her reason for being. I was confronted with the same dilemma others had to deal with. Asking people to pay for the opportunity to experience a sacred crystal skull didn't feel encouraged by it.

I had to find a way to deal with this inner conflict or place Compassion on a shelf with my personal crystal collection and close the door. I would be true to my deepest intentions for Compassion, as the sensitive Jane at the conference had instructed. Yet, I also felt obligated to share her with those who were ready to hear the true message of the crystal skulls today.

I discussed the matter with a friend who, as it turns out, became acutely sensitive to and close to Compassion. The first time Annie and I saw Phyllis she was behind a counter in a metaphysical bookshop. We were looking for something unusual in a card for a friend. Phyllis mentioned that she felt the crystals particularly strongly but admitted when I asked that she did not have any crystals of her own. I asked whether one had spoken to her in the store, and sure enough, she did have one that she said, resonated with her.

She showed it to me, and for some reason, I just told her I would buy it for her. I reasoned that she needed a personal crystal, and would pay me back someday, whenever she could get around to it. I didn't expect to be praised or repaid -- that was not my intention. I was just following my intuition.

Phyllis was very surprised and appreciative; Annie didn't get "weird" either. She stood back and just watched the drama unfold.

It just seemed the right thing to do, and, after all, crystals had been important to her. She was in contact with people new to crystals every day. Now she'd have firsthand experience to share with them of how it feels to know a certain crystal 24/7, and how it resonates with you, sending those "tingles" up your arm to the center of your head. What a delightful surprise for a truly sensitive person. I felt honored to meet and be able to help her.

Months later she thanked me again and insisted on repaying me for her crystal. I thanked her for thinking of me. After Phyllis, Annie, and I had become good friends, I asked her to manage my showing of Compassion.

"Take the money for admissions and private sessions please," I ask her. I didn't want to see it or even talk about it. Somehow, I felt guilty for charging money to experience a treasure that wanted to be shared by all. At the very beginning, when we were showing Compassion in our local area, I paid Phyllis a percentage, as if she were a member of my old fishing crew.

Phyllis explained that she has extraordinary sensitivity and is privileged to communicate with the crystals. She was perfect for the "job," as she could help protect Compassion. No doubt she and Annie had talked, and Annie had told her to watch Compassion when I get distracted talking to people. Talking to people about Compassion is what I believe I am here to do.

Annie could not do this all the time, as she was out of town much of the time caring for her elderly mother.
All the while, Annie was warming up to Compassion on her own. I could sense a deepening level of communication between Compassion and Annie. She started telling me more and more of what Compassion wanted and needed. What was I to do? To share the "Sacred Feminine" with a woman is a situation where a man, it seems, has to step back. (I was later to learn that this is not so; men just have to find the Sacred Feminine energy

85

within themselves and balance it with their Sacred Male.)

I began to see more deeply into the situation, letting Annie adjust to the new higher energy at her own speed. If only I were moving as fast! I would get intuitions and subtle "nudges," as I called them, but no direct communication. It just seemed that women would automatically resonate with Compassion; clearly, she touched their Sacred Feminine spirit in a most intimate way. They seemed to take this for granted and, with no background in skulls, were able to integrate.

I took some photos of the grid prior to the guests arriving at Katherine's. When I saw the photos later, they showed large orbs everywhere. One was caught right over the fourteen-and-a-half-inch Lemurian on the east end of the grid.

There was a sturdy old oak tree in the east, so our view of the moonrise would be delayed. As it worked out, I asked everyone to hold hands around the outside of the Lemurian grid. As the moon came into full view, the whole grid came alive. Moon glow poured through Compassion and then down though the thirteen Lemurians and to the outside circle of Lemurians. From there, Phyllis

said the light went straight up
and down!

As if on cue, Andrew and
Jenny stopped abruptly as the moon
shone through. I then asked my
guests, still holding hands, to
step inside the grid. It all
happened at once. As everyone
stepped in, not one person would
drop a hand. Everyone was still
bonded with the person next to
them -- truly a moment for all to
savor. This warmth, even at ten
o'clock on a chilly night, was
beautiful. **(Fig.4)**

Following an invocation by
Andrew, I asked Katherine to close
the outer grid and anchor it. Due
to an old leg injury, she had to
sit in a chair, but was able to
graciously close the ceremony.

We all just stood there,
feeling the energy vibrate through
us. It was one of the most
uplifting moments I have ever
experienced. The roughly fifteen
guests seemed to be frozen in
time. Standing there, eyes closed
or looking at Compassion, glowing
in the moonlight, I could see that
everyone was at peace. The vision
in my dream had been realized.
Elated, I knew that I was now part
of something far bigger than
myself, yet I had been able to
pull the parts together.

"Come up to Compassion if you wish," I finally said, revolving the turntable. I think if I hadn't interrupted the meditation, we would have been there for quite some time. There were probably thirty minutes of silence. Some said they saw Compassion change colors; Katherine saw her turn red and then give off a blue light, and the whole grid glowed a golden color.

It was a powerful event for me, and I am sure for others as well. There was no time limit. We finally broke it up two and a half hours later, as some were getting cold. We opened the grid and some left but most stayed, enjoying the moon glow and their inner experience, asking questions and visiting. I was exhausted by the time we packed up and left for home. It had been such a sublime experience, and I was relieved to know that all of it had flowed well and could see how many were touched by the experience.

PHOTOS

(Fig. 1)

Actual first photo of Compassion at
import Shop. Same "blazing eyes as in two
years of dreams. This photo was what made
me drive the four hundred miles to sit
and face this crystal skull.

PHOTOS

(Fig. 2)

Back of skull, showing the layering of quartz with Iron-Oxide between the first two layers of crystal. Coloring is a light beige with red Hematite border.

PHOTOS

(FIG. 3)

Annie at newly found end of table handing
out Mayan Calendars with attendee's
skulls for energizing and protection
while they shopped.

PHOTOS

(Fig.4)

Compassion on Dolphin Pedestal
with Lemurian Seed Crystals in
double circle. Notice Orbs in
background.

PHOTOS

(Fig.5)

Lemurian Sanctuary I created with
my crystals for Compassion with
Selenite lamps and large Citrine.

PHOTOS

(Fig.6)

Crystal Skull Compassion resting on Sacred Alter in forest grove on top of Mount Tamalpais, California.

LEMURIAN SANCTUARY

Chapter 9

While things were quiet, I got the strongest intuition to build a sanctuary for Compassion and my crystals. I had nowhere to do this, so I put an advertisement in the Ojai newspaper. What I got was people wanting to house my crystals and Compassion but limiting the time I could be with them. That wouldn't work.

I dreamed about it and took stock of what I had. I was living on an old boat. No room except for the dozen or so I always had around. My storage unit was only a ten by ten-foot space full of sail bags and spare parts. However, if I doubled the size and partitioned off half with a drop curtain, I could create a sacred sanctuary with shelves, and have my personal space that would be secure.

The very next day I went to my storage manager and asked to double my space. I moved all my existing stuff to the front half, and then got my tape measure and chalk. After surveying the area I'd have to work with, I went shopping. In addition to my original ten-by-ten space, I now had another of the same size for my new "sanctuary."

At the lumberyard, I found some cinderblocks and pine boards. I got about twenty-five cinderblocks and ten eight-foot pine boards. I bought a new carpet pad and carpeting.

I figured that after installing the shelving, I would be lying down in the center of a now eight-by-eight-foot space. I also found a wool blanket from Pendleton Woolen Mills, in Oregon. It was a Zuni medicine blanket with a large Hopi katsina doll on the front, with Apache and Hopi and other power symbols. Then I moved all crystals to the shelves. After two years of boxes only, I got motivated when I brought Compassion home. **(Fig.5)**

Annie was invited to come and help. She had stayed away, as it was my project, and she was just watching. When she got there, though, she took over arranging things. I figured this might happen and was pleased, as I wanted to share the experience.

I had to talk to someone; I was flying on autopilot, so to speak, and needed to touch the ground with Annie. I felt an especially strong connection with her in this. We would sit and just look at all the crystals I had mounted on teakwood stands. All the minerals I had for healing from years of collecting lined the sides, along with sixty other Lemurians that I used in grid work on the Zuni blanket.

When I felt it was complete, I was exceedingly happy with how it turned out. I'd eliminated much of the personal stuff I didn't need. I kept the things I needed for the boat, and memorabilia from past boats I've had. We had plenty of room to meditate now.

"Compassion is happy now." This is what I thought at the time. Then, after leaving her there for three days to acclimate to the other crystals, I brought her home, as I was missing her presence on the boat. For some reason, it seemed I didn't have the same connection with her! At this point, Annie reminded me that Compassion had asked for only three things: she didn't want to be submerged in water, she didn't want to be handled excessively and, last but certainly not least, she did not want to be in a dark warehouse! OOPS! I could see that the energy in Compassion was that of a woman; she was upset, and giving me the "silent treatment" after being left in the dark twenty-four hours a day, just as she had been in Africa.

I had to totally accept Compassion into my life now; she was becoming the center of it.

"It's not about you -- you have to drop your ego. It's about Compassion and *her* needs, and this is probably why she pursued you. She must have had faith in the purity of your intentions and the strength of your convictions," Annie told me.

"Good thing she wasn't drawn to my sensitivity," I joked. However, this turn of events worried me. Was I to be only an observer?

Prior to my purchasing Compassion and bringing her home, I happened to be in a local metaphysical book and crystal store, in my hometown.

I was teasing the owner about an extraordinarily large and beautiful polished citrine crystal sitting on a massive labradorite base, large enough for a light bulb to fit under the crystal. It was over eighteen inches tall and weighed over twenty pounds. I planned to offer what I believed was a fair price for it, as I thought if I spent the money on this magnificent crystal I would be satisfied, and not be tempted to pursue the crystal skull.

One day I was browsing in this store and happened to overhear the owner talking about slow business, and how she worried about paying the large rent that month. I took this as a cue and offered to buy the citrine for half of what she was asking. She gave me "the look" and accepted. The monster citrine was mine.

Now this extra-large polished citrine crystal occupies a position in the center of the sanctuary. Because of its calming and settling properties, it was my choice to energize Compassion's Sacred Place. It does not accumulate or allow any negative energy, and does not have to be cleared or programmed.

It is extremely stable, which is exactly what I wanted in the newly created "Lemurian Sanctuary," as I call it with over one hundred specimens. As a rule, I would clear and program all my crystals prior to placing them in the sanctuary as soon as I received them.

In the presence of this mighty citrine crystal, the group of Lemurians does not have to be cleared anymore unless "imprinted" by someone touching them. I was of course wondering what effect the Citrine had on Compassion.

I was thinking about how the metal roof and sides of the storage unit were holding in the white light. I felt the need to amplify the energy so it could "burst out" of this steel box. My wishes were answered when I came across a large fifteen-pound Lemurian cluster.

I happened to find this cluster, which is a very rare item in this size, at a very good price, and so added it to my collection. Now the sanctuary is finished. It has the Sacred Crystal Skull (when she visits), holding a place for those in her presence, and a prodigious citrine crystal to calm and balance the room. I needed an "explosion" of quartz powered by a cluster, something to radiate out all the energy being created in this space.

I know Compassion told Annie she didn't like to be in a dark warehouse anymore, so I kept her home with me and took her back to "her place" only when going there for meditation work. I hope this will clear things up between Compassion and me sometime in the future.

Outside would be the best place for her, exposing her to the sun and the moon, but this is what I have until the Universe sees fit to provide me with a safe place to create a new Lemurian Sanctuary for those who: See, Hear, and Feel in their hearts.

The sanctuary has provided me with a destination to walk to and get some exercise. I am retired and need to get out and walk. The time spent walking to the sanctuary was initially boring, but after doing some rearranging and an hour of meditation; it became exhilarating walking the mile back to the boat.

I talked to Annie about offering this sacred space to others who were close to Compassion. I called these people the "Family of Compassion." Every one called individually. Several of these people had contacted me about dreaming that a crystal skull with a movable jaw had literally flown across their bedroom at night -- and was all RED!

I had callers from as far away as British Columbia, Arkansas, Washington State, and Oregon, none knowing each other. I started organizing groups of people in the same area. The only thing I asked of them was to send me a write-up of their experiences. They were posted on my website under "People's Response to Compassion."

I usually do not speak about my experiences with Compassion, not presuming to be the spokesperson for her. However, I have to say that on one occasion, I actually did see Compassion flying past me when I was in a hypnagogic (half-awake) state late one night on the boat. I can't prove it, but am inclined to take these other people's word for it happening also.

Annie was not too happy about bringing anyone into the sanctuary. She felt it was my personal space and should be respected as such. I, on the other hand, had an overwhelming desire to share what I had done with others who resonated with Compassion. The compromise was that we would allow only a few "Compassion family" members to spend time there.

They were very appreciative of the experience, but I had a gut feeling that the location was not helping what I wanted to do as it was so private and therefore, could not be open to the public. I gave up on the idea and told Annie she was right. However, I do hope to find a situation where Compassion and all my crystals can be part of something larger that can be shared.

Reading James Redfield's book *The Celestine Prophecy;* I was deeply touched by how he was able to inspire personal evolutional growth in so many individuals. I was hoping with Compassion for this dynamic. They had a place called Viciente in the book. Later I saw the film and it brought tears to my eyes. I was so filled with unconditional love and peace that I knew that such a place was what I must have.

This was the Sacred Feminine, working with men and women to help them become the people that the Maya had prophesied, who will usher in the new energy to save the planet and our species.

I suppose this is what I was subconsciously trying to do with my little Lemurian Sanctuary and my desire to bring others to it.

CAMPING ON MOUNT SHASTA

Chapter 10

In November, I traveled north to camp on the sides of Mount Shasta with the Crystal Skull Compassion. Having lived in Alaska for twenty-four years, I was familiar with many mountains; this one, however, was truly memorable. I went there at the full moon to be alone with Compassion. Sitting by the campfire feeding it sticks, I watched the firelight do magical things to the foils, with reflections in Compassion. I felt the love and was reconnected with Compassion.

Gazing up from under the redwoods and seeing the moon peeking through the clouds and branches brought an eerie feeling. For a while, it looked like the moonlight was flashing on the ground like a strobe. It would be on Compassion, and then on me, and then dark. It reminded me of the months we spent camping outside while building a secure log cabin in the wilderness. One gets into the rhythms of Nature as she dictates one's patterns of waking and rest.

I was brought back to my current reality by a little rain

under the redwoods, but not enough
to go inside the tent I bought
that was too small for my six-
foot-three-inch frame. The rain
was just enough to bathe
Compassion in pure mountain
rainwater after being confined for
so long in Africa. I talked to her
in the moonlight and firelight,
which made her shift from
feminine-to masculine-looking. I
said I was sorry for being
thoughtless about leaving her in a
dark place.

It was a particularly
memorable night for Compassion and
me. It reminded me of moonlit
nights in Alaska, when a little
chill was in the air, and the
trees, swaying ever so slightly in
the wind, would whisper their
secrets to me. Then too, I
remember those flashes of
moonlight. This time I had a
companion with whom I was
attempting to make contact,
possibly even receive something
directly from her.

I was wondering how it would be
to have my drum to play, in the
way that Andrew had played his
shamanic drum. Next time I would
bring my drum. As the firelight
danced on Compassion's face, the
clouds finally disappeared, the
sky darkened, and we were alone.

At times like this, just
being alone with oneself and
watching a fire burn down in the
forest, even at a campground, can
help one find peace of mind. The
hard part is letting go of the
constant mental chatter going on,
and focusing on the sounds of the
forest and the snapping of the
fire. Compassion and I spent
quality time there, and I promised
to come back.

When I turned in, I suddenly
realized what a "Bigfoot" I really
am! Way too large for my adult-
size mountain tent, my feet were
out the door!

Two days later, I went
farther north to visit with an old
Alaskan fishing friend of mine,
John Swinnerton. We spent years
fishing king crab, herring, and
salmon back in the early
seventies. We'd shared some good
and bad times.

John is intelligent and likes
to expound on matters I can't
always follow. However, I listen
attentively anyway, figuring he
just needs to get it out, maybe to
sort things through in his mind.
Some people thought John talked
too much, probably because he was
talking way over their heads.
After getting seasick over the
side, he would put in a day's
work, equal to the strongest and

toughest man aboard. Later I hired him to run the deck of my own fishing boat.

I honestly didn't want the commitment of a fishing boat, and was happy making decent money while leaving the business stuff alone. I was living in a rustic log cabin on a friend's property. Back then there were several log cabins available for winter lodging, as it is better for a cabin to be heated in the winter so it won't get moldy and rot in the dampness.

We lived by a beautiful bay that we found by accident -- but that's a long story. Pushing around seven-hundred-and-fifty-pound crab pots on the pitching deck of a fishing boat in those waters took a very special kind of person.

John was still living in Ashland, Oregon, where he'd built his own recording studio. He is deeply involved in music, in recording, and in his own spiritual growth.

I wanted to place Compassion on his Light Connector that I had seen on my first visit with Stephanie. It was a frame work that held an Icosahedron and Decahedron intertwined into one form. With a copper wire mesh on the floor and copper tubing held by people sitting inside the frame; they were also connected the object considered by John to be a sacred geometrical form. I wanted to share Compassion with John, as he had been instrumental in my decision to buy her. I also wanted to meet his new friend, Bunny. I had heard that Bunny worked with her skull "Ming" to connect with this device, and I wanted to see what kind of results we would get collectively. This would connect us all to Compassion.

Bunny is an extraordinarily powerful shaman woman he had met, a healer who could travel to the Underworld to work with the causes of someone's illness. She was the "real thing," he said.

Bunny had spent time on a commune in Vermont, working on an organic hydroponic garden project and harvesting maple syrup.

After Stephanie and I had visited, before bringing Compassion home in August, Bunny had come to John wanting to work with him and his Light Connector with her newly found green hematite skull.

John and I discussed some personal matters, including how I was uncomfortable with asking for money to share Compassion. He told me to go with my heart and not to

focus on the money. If I were
being called by the entity located
in this crystal skull (or beyond),
then it was my destiny to follow.
The very shape of a skull is
sacred geometry itself. "The skull
is the resonating chamber of the
brain, so it has the frequency of
the brain it held," he said.

I was taken right away by how
direct Bunny was, not a "chit
chat" kind of woman. She was
charming but direct, and with no
pretense. Bunny had become a
serious woman on a spiritual
quest. She said her beautiful
green skull was called "Ming."
She'd found it in an import store
in Barbados. The owner told her it
was a relic from the Ming Dynasty.
It looked almost black but, in the
light, a deep green came out.

We spent time in the Light
Connector, each of us having
different reactions to the skulls.
I saw all green in my mind's eye.
John saw visions of Compassion
flying by him through the air, and
a green glow from Ming. Bunny
didn't comment.

I could see that my friend was
acutely sensitive to the skulls,
as it was a long time before he
got back to us. Bunny explained
that he needed to be grounded.
She'd placed Ming with Compassion

so that they could download information between them.

Later, when it was dark, John wanted to experiment with different lighting under Compassion, so we gathered around her. John used some bright LED strobe lights that he had used on his Light Connector. We tried all different spectrums of light until we came to blue. At this point the whole room lit up. It was as if none of the other lights had any effect at all.

The whole room pulsed with this bright blue light; we had to look away. Bunny even covered her eyes. I was seeing the side of Compassion's skull and watching the room pulsate with this intensity.

John was on the floor, looking Compassion directly in the eyes about two feet away from her, and stayed there for what seemed like at least fifteen minutes. Finally, Bunny cried out!

"Turn the light off!" It took some shaking and yelling to bring John back. He finally reached over and turned the little blue light off.

Eyes wide open and apparently unable to hear us, John was stunned. He said later, after Bunny had worked to ground his aura and, with her hands, to calm him down and bring him back, that he'd assumed he'd be able to handle the energy after ten years of intense study and meditation.

"I was unprepared for the level of energy or the depth I was traveling -- so much happening at once," he said.

We called it a night. For my part, I was still "buzzing" with high-energy feelings, as if I had been next to a high-voltage transformer. My hair was standing on end and I was shaking ever so slight.

The experience unsettled me. I didn't want any harm to come to John, as a result of using a strobe to stare into the eyes of this crystal skull. Compassion has extreme depth in her left eye. One group wanted to do an I-MAX film traveling through her left eye on a big screen. One can go inside and as the film person experienced. Her right eye has several foils and therefore, cannot be penetrated so easily however, this is where the blazing eye dreams for me came from.

OJAI HOUSE-SHOWING

Chapter 11

After a brief visit, I
decided to head home, as John was
scattered and not focused at all.
Bunny said she'd not received
anything from Compassion as her
eyes were closed, and she was
protecting herself the whole time.
Later I learned she'd spent time
with John, mending his aura;
unable to handle overexposure to
the energy, it had been "torn."

She said she'd successfully
mended it, in a way similar to
sewing it up, and that he was
"fine now." As for me, I am much
the wiser for his experience. *This
is an interesting woman,* I told
myself. Still, I was concerned
about John. Bunny said not to
worry, assuring me that her work
on him had done the job. Woman of
few words, this one.

I felt that moonlight was the
connection I shared with
Compassion. I'd had my zodiac
chart done by old Alaskan friend
who had a powerful computer and
software. She told me I was a

"triple" Cancer. I'd been on the ocean for the past forty-plus years, and I loved the moonlight in any setting. Whether on the ocean or filtering through the canopy of the forest trees, it is like being bathed in a silver essence.

Therefore, that is why I celebrate my commitment to Compassion every full moon night. I start by letting her bask in the sunlight, but not enough to get her too hot.

This time, the reflections coming back from Compassion were magenta, and the beams of light passing through her were magenta and lime green. I was concerned; the three layers of quartz might separate as they expand at different rates and the air bubble in water between layers could also expand at a different rate and cause pressure on the fissure. Due to the unique properties of this particular crystal skull, I can never be too careful.

Showing Compassion at a metaphysical store, I was discussing her when a clerk looked at the back of Compassion's skull and casually remarked, "She has an enhydro bubble in the back of her head!"

"What?" I said in bewilderment. Sure enough, if you look closely right above where Compassion's pineal gland would have been located in the center of the brain, you can see a one-millimeter air bubble. The clerk then asked me to hold the skull and rock it up and down. "It moves!" she confirmed.

I was once again amazed at how women are so comfortable with Compassion. Her statement had been so matter-of-fact that I had to file it away to "shout out" later.

Ever wanting to show Compassion to people, I asked a metaphysical place in Ojai, but they asked more to rent the space than I thought we would be able to make from small donations and small showings.

When we found the Ojai House, it was like a gift from heaven. What a beautiful place! It had a huge deck in the back with an old oak right in the center.

The owner, Megan (Nutmeg, as she is known by many friends), was highly receptive to having us do our showing of Compassion in the back. Meg is a friend of our friend Phyllis, so that made it easy. She agreed to take a percentage of what we got at the entrance door, so it was exceedingly easy to work with her.

I made posters, and Phyllis got a group of friends to put them up all around Ojai. I was still having trouble about the money, feeling a bit guilty to charge for something I felt was here for all to experience. Times were hard, and I was concerned that lack of money would keep people away. I felt this very keenly. I myself had been out of work for over two years with the knee surgeries, etc., and had experienced a very tight budget.

The showing was immensely successful. I would guess eighteen to twenty people came. All loved the place, and there were some who spoke of a very famous skull named MAX. I had never seen it, but heard it was five layers of quartz and cloudy, whereas Compassion had three layers and was clear. One woman from Mexico City who had been with the Mitchell-Hedges

Skull said she felt a totally different kind of energy from Compassion -- subtle, with a feminine energy that warmed her heart.

Of course, this is all subjective. Everyone will have his or her own personal experience. However, people like Gerald, Phyllis, and John are physically moved in her presence. Phyllis will jump whenever I turn Compassion on her turntable, even with her back turned to her. She says she feels waves that are strong enough to push her!

I recalled John's words about the human skull being the resonating chamber for the brain. Once the brain is removed, the skull still resonates with the old mental content, or, as some believe, it can be used to channel other entities that have the power to come into our plane of existence through this now crystal resonating chamber. Maybe it's the sacred geometry that makes this possible? He has studied the matter exhaustively and can explain it well.

Quartz crystal piezoelectric, it will hold and, under the proper conditions (i.e., given a slight electrical charge or being stuck with another piece of Quartz) give off an electrical charge. In a darken room, strike the bottoms of two separate pieces of quartz. You will see sparks and a light given off. Our brains are wired for electrical impulses, so it follows that if we can attune to the frequency of the quartz crystal skull, the information would be both received and stored. Think about it how could a quartz crystal give off electricity if it didn't store it? Then too, aren't our memories and thoughts "electrical?" in nature?

As I was thinking earlier, if the hematite and iron oxide at the back of Compassion are truly magnetic, then she is giving off a slight electrical charge continually. The reason the ancients used quartz crystal as a medium in which to carve the skulls could very well be that it not only represents thought transference, "thinking," but can also serve as a spiritual computer in which massive amounts of knowledge could be permanently stored as long as the integrity of the skull is maintained.

Once the skull or quartz point is broken, or some random quartz pieces are melted down and poured into a mold, its properties change. The sacred geometry is still present, but the integrity of the skull or naturally grown quartz is lost. Compassion has three separate layers. Why not then extrapolate that they were used by the carver and later the programmer to house different levels of information? They are different compartments, after all.

Some believe it's all about the entity inside the skull to determine the characteristics; might skulls with several layers house different entities? People see different faces in Compassion. A photo of Compassion taken on a light box using a "white" light bulb shows her in a deep golden color. Another image is of what seems to be a horse skull with a massive headdress. And there is one that appears to be an ancient Egyptian baboon. When the skull is in normal light, this area is clear as water. I have been able to duplicate these photos. I am asking others more sensitive than I for information.

Many agree that they feel Sacred Feminine energy in Compassion, a holy spirit like Mary Magdalene's or the bodhisattva Guan Yin's kind of energy that is the pinnacle of mercy, kindness, nurturing, and unconditional love. All of these qualities they feel in Compassion's presence.

Annie and Phyllis took over the arrangement of Compassion; I just stood back and watched. I was exceedingly pleased that Annie took such an interest. Phyllis was enjoying her also.

I only record what other people say. I do not want a conflict of interest, so I try to stay objective and let them speak for themselves as I tell people, "Compassion speaks for herself." However, I don't always keep my opinions to myself.

I used to tell people. "I am just the feet. My job is to create an event, and bring Compassion. As her guardian, I stay close so none can inadvertently harm her." This has almost happened twice now within the past year.

During the middle of the program in Ojai, California, a latecomer, a young man, approached Compassion after I'd invited people to come up and have a closer look at her. They were especially interested in the iron-oxide occlusion in the back of her skull, as this one-of-a-kind feature distinguishes her from all other crystal skulls in the world.

It was the second time someone (again a male) had tried to pick up Compassion, evidently thinking it was a solid skull with a face carved into a crystal. He was so surprised the jaw didn't come up with the skull that he almost dropped it, as the weight is all in the back, and out of balance. I saw the eyes of other guests get quite large, as they recognized what was happening.

"Please do not touch the skull!" I shouted, swinging around in time to grab Compassion just as his hands were slipping from her. At over ten pounds, and counterbalanced by the heavier cranium, she is not easy to hold. Compassion gets extremely wet from condensation from people's hands, as she is quartz and is the temperature of the air, which is generally cooler than our body temperature. Quartz assumes the temperature of the air or water around it, taking time to accommodate to its environment. Like a reservoir of water, it always finds the ambient temperature.

When you hold a quartz crystal, it will be cool to the touch, but after a while, it will warm up to your body temperature. If you then drop it into a glass of ice water, it could shatter, as it cannot contract to the coldness fast enough. The same is true of the opposite situation. If you do not prepare for this unexpected condensation, it is a surprise, and the crystal is likely to slip from your grip. Evidently, he hadn't heard my announcement at the beginning of the program:

"Please not touch Compassion, as she is extremely fragile." I think he came in late. I told him

she could be felt without
touching, as the experience of hot
spots from a distance of about
eight inches for most, and farther
outward for others, depending on
the person. There was of course no
fault or blame for this poor chap;
he was embarrassed, and his
intention had not been malicious.
Still, he got plenty of "vibes"
from the others in the crowd. I
wanted to talk to him, but he left
rather abruptly -- too bad. I had
wanted to console him and explain
the situation with people and
Compassion.

This was the second time
Compassion had been in harm's way
while under my protection. I was
shaken up. How could I have been
so careless! I couldn't bear to
have anything happen to her under
my watch! After who knows how long
it has been since she was carved,
for her to be damaged in any way,
or for her jaw to be broken in an
accident would be unforgivable.

I know there is a force out
there that would want Compassion
destroyed, a force that does not
want her message of the Sacred
Feminine to touch us all I am

told. There are forces that want
to maintain their hold on the
consciousness of man, and keep us
living in fear and therefore, easy
to contol.

A recurring theme throughout
history is for those who would
find higher consciousness within
themselves -- "the Kingdom of
Heaven" -- to be silenced or
killed. Sometimes I think I may be
becoming paranoid, but that's my
job -- I'm a Guardian -- and I
take it extremely seriously.

As a retired fisherman and
mariner, I remember well those
nights when the exhausted crew was
asleep, confident that an
appointed crew member would be
diligent on his watch. All were
secure in knowing that the boat
was on course, and that they
wouldn't awaken to the sound of
crashing waves or grinding rocks.
This is how I spent twenty years
of my life, and is possibly one
reason Compassion chose me as her
caretaker and guardian.
For all my experience, though, I
must yet tighten my watch!

The fact is that I was not
chosen because I am especially

"spiritual." This admission takes a load off me! I don't have to pretend to be something I am not. I've seen some fellow caretakers affecting spirituality and wisdom, perhaps trying to validate the power of their skulls, and it looks like quite a strain! It makes life much easier that people who are sensitive can feel Compassion even before I take her out of her protective carrying case.

It has been my experience that touching her or holding her will not give one a stronger impression. Simply holding your hand several inches from her, especially toward the back, you will find hot places. When you find your place, you can "pull" the energy outward.

However, I am not the one to make policy. If the person has the need to touch Compassion I will let my intuition make the decision for me. People like Carole Davis and Leandro de Souza are above reproach in my opinion. They are only interested in subjective study and therefore, I feel, have

no agenda other than what has been
implied.

I do still bathe Compassion in
Sea Water when I get home, then
fresh water to wash off the
abrasive salt crystals and let her
dry in Sunlight.


PEOPLE'S RESPONSE TO COMPASSION


Chapter 12

Right after the last showing at
the Ojai House, I got an email
from a man named Robert. He said
he had seen a poster for the
showing, but even though he was in
town he had missed it. He said he
was extremely keen on seeing
Compassion, as he had had an
unusually intense dream about her.

I agreed to meet with him and
Phyllis at Katherine Rosengren's
home in Ventura. I wanted
Phyllis's opinion as well as
Katherine's, a woman who is also
very sensitive.

We met Robert, a serious young writer who lives in Berkeley. He told us he was just finishing up his book on lucid dreaming. The experience he described to us was incredible. Slowly turning the turntable and observing Compassion from all sides, he spoke of his dreaming about Compassion and what had brought him to us.

Robert wrote the following when I asked him, as I do all those who have the eyes to see and ears to hear, to please write me about their experiences:

"*The crystal skull named Compassion by its present caretaker, came into my life from a dream, quite literally on the wing of the reddest dawn I have ever seen. This was January 9, 2010. The dream followed another that had been mostly mundane, and was quite startling.*

*I found myself standing in the presence of a large glowing red skull. A holographic array emanated from its eyes and arched out and upwards in a fan-like display. Within the field, a Phoenix rose and began to spread*

*its wings. Then, I awoke. The
entire room and everything in it
was suffused and lit up by this
incredible red dawn glow. I gazed
at it all for a few moments, then
went back to bed."*

The remainder is on the
website I created to chronicle
people's experiences with
Compassion in their own words.
http://www.crystalskull-
compassion.com/ Peoples-Response-
to-Compassion. This information
was certainly unusual, as
Compassion had originally come to
me in a dream also. Robert, as I
said, is an intensely pragmatic
and serious person and had not
seen Compassion "live" until this
meeting.

Katherine and Phyllis both
took this quite seriously. I asked
Robert to chronicle his
experiences and dreams for my
website, here is what he shared:

*"Everyone introduced
themselves, and I sat down in
front of Compassion. When I did, I
saw that she was emanating a field
of energy about twenty or so feet
in diameter around us. An intense
feeling of déjà vu washed through
me and was accompanied by a rush*

of energy from foot to throat chakras. This slowly settled down into a somatic bliss that lingered in my sensorium for many hours afterwards.

Being near Compassion evokes pure joy in the receiver, and I believe this to be a universal phenomenon, at least from my limited exposure to her.

Over the course of the following two weeks I had several dreams and direct visions of Compassion, or related to her. After careful examination of these experiences, I believe she has come out of the darkness to aid in the reactivation of the various planetary chakra centers and vortex energy, locally and around the globe, to raise the vibratory rates of sentient beings everywhere.

As to the purpose of such an undertaking, the meaning is both implicit and explicit, according to the awareness and understanding of each individual. The true nature of Compassion expresses itself through the basic idea of custodianship and all its myriad and attendant responsibilities.

*The present time is one of both crisis and chaos, and because of such a state of affairs, there is an incredible opportunity to effect massive change, for the old zeitgeist is crumbling and no longer serves us. It is my hope that all who encounter Compassion will rise to the challenge that her very existence and presence in the world portends: Raise your awareness and purify your intentions. The world doesn't need to be saved, it needs to be truly lived upon and nurtured."*

Robert's other dreams are on the website given above.

Katherine saw an image of Guan Yin rising from the top of Compassion, Phyllis saw a beam of white light, also emanating from Compassion's head.

I was anchoring the field created around us, grounding it to Earth. As a rule, I don't see visions, but tried to make myself useful. It reminded me of my days of running a fishing boat in Alaska. I learned to surround myself with intelligent people – that is, once I got over my EGO getting in the way! I had the experience of being on the water, while they had the chance to be part of the larger decision making. Their input of things I could not follow then was such an asset. We all worked together for the common good.

I still had the final say and ultimate responsibility, but if I disagreed I would respect them enough to tell them why! I was surely wrong sometimes. This is the biggest hurdle to overcome: the captain is not always right.

As I draw on this past experience, I cannot afford to be wrong in my handling of Compassion, so the people whom Compassion and I have come in contact with over the short time she has been in my care are all dear to me. Synchronicity has brought us together, and I am thankful. Nothing is happening by sheer chance now, as people in Oregon, Arizona, California, Washington State, Brazil, South Africa, and Canada all contact me.

Encouraging them to speak, recording their insights and visions, is creating a vision of Compassion from the very people

she attracts. Without their input,
I don't think I could stay
objective. One truly intuitive
psychic on the East Coast named
Susan wrote me after doing a
remote reading on Compassion.

"To those with ears to hear,
and eyes to see, and with hearts
to feel, they will come!" I was
told this by a sensitive woman
named Susan who received
information from Compassion. I
resonate with this thought and use
it often to describe the people
drawn to Compassion in dreams or
by chance through a search engine
request for Compassion.

I am still in touch with
Robert. He and Phyllis joined me
on a vortex hunt we'd heard would
be happening on the Ventura River.
It is used by the Chumash Indians.
We placed Compassion in a small
grid, and meditated for a while.
It was peaceful but with too many
people to let me be comfortable,
so we walked back to the car.

Those who are drawn by the
Crystal Skull Compassion,
including Robert, Phyllis, and
Katherine, and all who personally
have had experiences with

Compassion, are my new friends and crystal skull family. Compassion is totally different from any other skull in the world, and only the Mitchell-Hedges skull matches this beautiful sculpture. Today, however, the world's best copiers are hard at work, trying to mass-produce skulls from every material. People are willing to "create" a skull history to improve sales.

This is the way of capitalism; it is who we are as a nation. No one's to blame if it's all one knows.

I would suggest that people get a hold of a reputable outlet or artist, like Stones of Brazil or Leandro de Souza, if they wish to acquire a contemporary crystal skull that is an authentic carving. The energy in the skull is a combination of the properties of an original piece of material and the sacred geometry of the shape of the skull itself.

Having to add lead to poured quartz stops the bubbles and makes GLASS! The thing to remember is, the clearer a skull, the more likely it is glass. This is only

my humble opinion; let your
intuition be your guide. I have a
"Skull Vodka" bottle that is made
of high-quality glass. I don't get
anything out of it once the vodka
is gone. I rest my case. You be
the judge.

In February, I went back to
the Ojai House for another
showing. Meg the proprietor is a
sweetheart and was again easy to
work with. A crystal wholesaler
who had two tables of crystals and
minerals for sale happened to be
there also.

Annie was with me this time.
We offered the private session
with Compassion only, no
presentation. I wanted to see how
that would work out. We have no
place to do this work, as we have
no room where we live.

At the end of each session, I
didn't have the heart to charge
people for the experience of
Compassion. I could feel these
people were answering a deep-
seated need or calling to be with
Compassion. It was too much for
me. I told them it was a blessing
from Compassion to them.

They all went away happy, and some I could see were relieved; now they could buy lunch.

"I didn't charge them, but I will pay you anyway," I told Meg the owner when it came time for me to settle up with her. Meg gave me the warmest smile and a soul-felt hug and whispered in my ear: "I wasn't going to charge you anyway."

I would prefer to just do presentations and have people come up for a private moment with Compassion afterwards, but that takes too long and some feel they don't get enough time for themselves. They are, therefore, willing to pay for personal time. And at this point, it becomes business.

I will of course reach a dead end when my resources run out. I am not a wealthy man; however, the time I had been doing free presentations in Ventura, San Diego, Ojai, Ashland, Oregon, and Yarnell, Arizona, made me feel rich indeed.

I have surrendered my work and myself with Compassion to the Universe. I feel that my destiny

is to share her with as many as
may need her. This is why she has
come to me. As mentioned earlier,
this is all new to me; I have no
background to fall back on, so
will just have to see how it works
out. When I told Compassion I was
no longer going to charge for
presentations, I had my hand just
above her. The warmth I felt lit
up my entire upper body. So I know
that on one level we have made
contact; however, there are other
issues that still have to be
addressed.

SCIENTIST EXAMINES COMPASSION

Chapter 13

Eager to learn about
Compassion's genesis, I made an
appointment with Dr. Ray Corbett,
Associate Curator of Archaeology
at the Museum of Natural History

in Santa Barbara. I had contacted Dr. Corbett to see whether he might be interested in studying a crystal skull.

I sent two pictures of Compassion to him. He responded by setting a date and asking whether he could invite a colleague of his, Dr. John Minch, a geologist-paleontologist, to join us. I happily agreed, saying that I was looking for a professional opinion on the carving of the skull, as well as its properties.

I invited Phyllis to accompany me to the museum. My motive was to have a witness and someone especially sensitive to the people around her. I wanted her take on the scientists' reactions, comparing their feelings with my own. Phyllis is a remarkably empathic woman and is very close to Compassion.

I want to make it clear I am not quoting these people a they wish not to be and I respect this.

When we arrived, Dr. Corbett asked whether they could examine Compassion in the presence of his archeology class. I declined because I wanted the geologist and archeologists complete attention to the task at hand. I knew that students asking questions would only distract them and me. I wanted to keep track of their findings and asked Phyllis to take notes. We agreed to share Compassion with the class after the examination was completed.

I have to say I felt trepidation concerning the examination of Compassion by the scientist. Not that I found anything wrong with her, but just knowing that the goal of science is to prove beyond a shadow of doubt with repeatable physical evidence seems somehow out of sync with the subtleties of Compassion.

The Scientific Method makes no allowances for metaphysical properties or anything that doesn't fit into accepted scientific paradigms. Dating and method of the carving of this skull is the issue today. I wasn't looking for proof of Compassion being ancient, as I knew they had no way of telling.

I was put at ease right away by the professional manner in which the examination was conducted. Dr. Corbett introduced us to Dr. Minch, and described his vast background in geology and gemology. As it turns out, he belonged to the same gem and mineral society, in Ventura, that Annie and I had joined some years back to play with the rock-cutting wheels. I remember those old rock hounds didn't like to work with quartz. I didn't understand when I asked to cut a cabochon out of quartz and they all said.

"You don't want to use that. It's too brittle and will break too easily."

To the best of my knowledge, the Museum of Natural History in Santa Barbara didn't have an electron microscope, or any of the weird things one sees on TV, with flashing lights and tanks of some mysterious fluid to find specific gravity of a skull like the Mitchell-Hedges skull.

I questioned whether the process of examining the Mitchell-Hedges skull at Hewlett-Packard was mainly for show, and how much actually came down to cutting against the axis of a particular piece of quartz. I asked Drs.

Minch and Corbett if I could quote
their findings on my website.

They had done their homework
as they looked for grinding marks.
I told them about the palate area
where some polishing marks were
still present. They went there and
spent some time. In addition, they
told me that what I had called the
rock matrix was iron oxide that
had seeped between layers as the
original quartz crystal and become
encapsulated when cooling. They
called it an "iron-oxide
occlusion."

Dr. Minch also found what I
called the "enhydro bubble." They
didn't comment on that, but Dr.
Minch did ask me to rotate the
skull up and down so he could see
whether the bubble moved. It did.
He was excited now! I never
mentioned that it had been
discovered earlier.

Up to this time, they seemed
reserved, but seeing that I had no
agenda, they now relaxed, and were
busy chatting back and forth. What
I got was that when the iron oxide
(hematite)"seeped" between the
layers of quartz, A bubble of air
was trapped in solution,

presumably water, and was encapsulated, along with the occlusion.

"The skull was found in Africa, and possibly in the Brandberg Mountains." I said. He didn't have any idea where the quartz had come from and did not comment.

During the examination Phyllis was sitting back, observing the scene. I told her earlier it would be a challenge for me to keep quiet and not go on about all the things I saw and thought about the skull. I told them their expert information was what I was there for, and that I wanted the good with the bad.

They took the jaw and carefully set it aside. The jaw has been cut from the same crystal as the skull was the contention. However, they did not think the jaw was cut directly from the skull as I thought.

"A foil that starts above the right temple runs directly through the skull and through the jaw; this suggests to me that the jaw was cut directly from the skull." I said. I had to speak up, also,

at the front of the skull there is
a large foil that runs through the
front teeth and at the bite makes
a 45-degree turn that continues
through the lower teeth into the
jaw. My contention is that this
fracture happened during
separation of jaw from skull.

Dr. Minch held his chin and
thought for a while, considering
my logic. The two scientists
looked at each other. This seemed
to fall on deaf ears, they were
extremely polite and didn't want
to argue with me. I have to
applaud them in there
professionalism. I get to
emotional at times.

I said nothing and we let it
go, as we could not see eye to eye
on the subject. Dr. Minch also
found golden titanium "hairs"
called rutile. This was in the
skull in three-meter hairs that
are the same length in the jaw.

Today, cutting against the
axis of the quartz could not be
done with contemporary grinders,
as it would surely fracture. On
the skull's cranium, there are
three different fracture marks
where the quartz comes together in

layers. Running a fingernail along them is possible as they are clear to the surface and go around the top of the skull.

I'd gotten no definitive answer, so I changed tacks. "As a lapidary, could YOU cut a skull like this with today's modern machines?" I asked. Silence. After scratching his chin, he looked at Dr. Corbett. and reflected how difficult it would be and how long it would take to accomplish this.

So, this is where we left it. No commitment. They had volunteered that it was cut by hand, so it really wasn't an issue. I was there to get their professional opinions but not necessarily assume the "accepted scientific position." I appreciated the clear demonstration we were having.

Dr. Minch didn't think this skull was machine-made. He made me aware of lobes in the back of the skull that are not uniform; the skull is asymmetrical. I saw front teeth area, maxilla, is at an angle to its right. When the jaw is replaced, it's not so evident, but when removed it is obvious the upper teeth angle to the right. I was speechless! I'd never noticed this!

I showed them what appears to be the only polishing marks we found are on the palate. He agreed this showed where a hand literally bounced over areas where a machine would have cut them smoothly

Dr. Minch, who is a leader in his field with the highest of professional standards, had examined Compassion in detail. I thanked him for his thoroughness and he left with a warm handshake and the best of wishes for our future with Compassion.

Dr. Corbett took us across the museum grounds to his lab class. His students were busy cataloguing when we arrived. I found a place to display Compassion and the class of about eighteen asked to take photos.

We said our good-byes and thanked them for their generous time and expertise. We left with all kinds of things to talk about. Phyllis congratulated me on keeping my mouth, mostly, shut! We laughed at the impasse reached when all of us could plainly see where the jaw had been cut from the skull. This was a real head-scratcher for all of us. All in all, it was a truly memorable experience.

Since that time, my response and attitude toward being the new caretaker and guardian of a crystal skull has changed quite a bit. At first, I regarded Compassion as simply part of my established crystal collection, and had no real intentions for her.

That was August 6, 2009; now, in February 2011, while I have not taken the time to reflect on the changes the whole experience has made in me personally, I believe I am living them.

Now, two years and many presentations and realizations later, I am still not a psychic medium, although many skull caretakers seem to be today. I am content to let Compassion speak for herself. I have learned to accept and appreciate people who have come into my life through the Crystal Skull Compassion.

I respect them all, understanding that they have their

own compelling reasons to be around Compassion. I am tremendously blessed indeed to have such kind and sensitive people to advise me and have patience with my somewhat unusual spontaneous manner.

These are people who of their own free will have given their time and traveled distances to assist me in my desire to understand this beautiful, human-looking, sculpted quartz crystal work of art.
I am following their lead. Taking advice as I go. Had it been all about my ego, greed, or desire for personal power, this unusual crystal skull would surely not have called me!

FEAR OF FALLING SHORT

Chapter 14

This is my feeling now. The new Renaissance of Enlightenment is upon us. We can choose to let go of our lower vibrational desires of the ego and move up through our energy centers to higher frequencies, recognizing ourselves as the "Star Beings" (for lack of a better secular term) that we really are.

Compassion is the answer! Simple! Having compassion means treating one another, as we would like to be treated, with unconditional love, nurturing, and respect. Most holy people have taught and exemplified this Golden Rule in one way or the other and, after millennia of wrongdoing, it's time that we did the same.

I am not exempt by any means, I have the same lessons to learn, opening my heart to those around me.

As we hurtle through space on this "Garden of Eden" planet, it is our duty and privilege to show compassion for one another.

We have to acknowledge that the planet will survive without us: we don't have to "save" it --

we have to save ourselves! As Robert said, "We have to nurture her and learn to live with Mother Earth, not despite her." But enough of this sermon! You either get it or you don't!

No person or organization is selling absolution. It is all up to you! You have to make the conscious decision to change the way you look at your fellow beings, and the planet.

That's where free presentations with the Crystal Skull Compassion come in. I don't want to sound clichéd, but after the epiphany that started me collecting crystals, and that stopped as suddenly as it had begun, and then after spending a significant portion of my retirement on a crystal skull, I feel that my path is very clear. I am becoming an instrument that is part of something immeasurably bigger than me. The pieces of the large puzzle are coming together.

Living in the woods of Alaska and building two log cabins, I learned serenity. In this peaceful environment I worked through my anger issues surrounding the futility of the Viet Nam conflict and how I was treated upon my return home. Losing two properties my former wife and I had hewn from the Alaskan wilderness by hand, only to have them taken away from us by bureaucrats, was something we were not prepared to handle.

Alaska will tame any man. Alaska will welcome his negative attitude and subsequent anger, and temper it by his simple struggle through his first hard winter in the wilderness. I, for one, had become acutely aggressive as a fisherman, pushing for everything I had. Back in 1969, I was being led not by compassion, but by my EGO and fear of failure.

Under great financial pressure of responsibility for my fishing boat, new family members, and a crew to consider, my anger surged in a last-ditch effort to court financial success. I was hard on myself and everyone around me. Naturally, that approach failed, but I actually did learn something -- the hardest way -- from living in the woods. Getting up earlier and staying later and working

harder than my competitors would
be my means.

This attitude, though brought
on by lack of confidence, finally
resolved itself when I found
balance with my very talented
crew. I didn't have to be a
Captain Bligh. There are many
Captain Blighs in the fishing
industry, and they are all afraid.
I learned to ease up on my ego
demands and allowed others in.
These were extremely fast-paced
times in the Alaskan fisheries.
Fortunes were being made from
split-second decisions and much
risk-taking. I found that a team
that was totally invested in our
mutual success could contribute
immensely in the decision-making
without stripping the captain of
his self-respect.

My career improved immensely
to the point where I was in the
premier salmon fishery in Alaska
with two experienced sons, both
ready to continue my legacy and
send themselves through college,
then possibly pass the now
million-dollar operation on to
their own children.

It all came crashing down with the Exxon Valdez oil spill. I was working my sons into the business; my elder son was working as a fully paid member of the crew, and my younger son was helping his mother on a salmon set net site on the island we lived on, in a place called Halibut Cove, Alaska.

I lost everything that was important to me, including my family. When the money goes, the relationship is not far behind, I learned. I had to downsize, as I worked only three months a year. I sold my entire fishing business for pennies on the dollar to -- of all people -- a person working at the Valdez oil pumping dock!

Meanwhile, the press was advertising "Blackened Salmon," as we were allowed to fish during the oil spill, in the same areas. We destroyed our markets and our credibility to downplay the seriousness of one of the most devastating oil spills in America's history. I did manage to get a permit and boat in a local gillnet fishery closer to home in the Cook Inlet region. I wanted to be with close friends and my younger son. My eldest was very capable and independent; he was fishing with a friend.

This lasted two years, until the sport fishing industry displaced this 100-year-old staple of the Alaskan economy. Now they are allowing the "snagging" of sockeye salmon by people standing shoulder to shoulder on the riverbanks. (Sockeye eat krill; so will not take a lure.)

It displaces the old fishery but increases the income of local businesses and others who have moved in to take advantage of this formerly illegal windfall. Set nets that traditionally had to go dry in the low tide to be legal, were also now allowed out two hundred yards beyond low-tide lines. (I believe that is the distance.) The point is that the new rules and outside boundaries all but eliminated this magnificent fishery. Once again, I had to move.

The area we were forced into was such a small place that thirty-foot tides would wash a boat over the line, and then the "fish cops" would be waiting there to confiscate our catch and write a hefty fine! I sold out again, getting the message. Alaskan fisheries were rapidly being downsized to make way for smaller boat fisheries.

This time I left Alaska for good, my heart broken. After twenty hard years, the loss of everything had taught me humility. I took it all as my karmic lesson in humility.

I found myself sleeping next to a smelly, hot diesel engine in an old tugboat. I was running a converted WW2 landing craft on a seismic retrofit of the Bay Bridge in San Francisco for a bridge company after the Loma Prieta earthquake. I couldn't afford a motel as all my money was going to child support and credit-card debt.

I still had my Merchant Marine captain's license to help me find work. These were hard times for me, but nothing was as painful as losing the time with my sons.

Throughout the time that I spent with my sister Stephanie in

Carmel, I asked the Universe for abundance. Then my mother died prematurely, and I received a portion of her estate. The coinciding of her death and my inheritance with my request for abundance brought me some uneasy feelings." I began to think, "Everything we receive must come at a price, and it all comes to balance."

Meeting Annie again after 30 years was, I feel, brought about by me returning to an old oak tree. I used to play in this tree next to the Little Sur River when I was about nine years old. Now, I was drawn back to be comforted, and to ask the being I have come to call "The Father of the Forest" for his help.

With tears running down my cheeks, I asked for a partner. I wanted a life mate who was worldly, kind, capable, and self-sufficient. The last thing I asked for was a sign that she was on her way to me, that her name would be Annie. It just came to me.

Late one evening two weeks later, I was in a restaurant in Carmel with my sister. Earlier that evening, all dressed up in a new suit and with $40.00 in my pocket, I had shown up at a class reunion cocktail party -- one week early! Such is the life of a dyslexic!

Stephanie was in bed when I got back. I explained what had happened, and we both had to laugh, not surprised, as dyslexic people seem to have little concept of time.

I asked if she would be kind enough to get up and get dressed, so I could console myself with a glass of wine and a night out in Carmel. We decided to go to Toot's Lagoon, a popular restaurant. Stephanie was aware of how down in the dumps I was, so she agreed to get up, get dressed, and do all the things a woman does before going out. God Bless my sister!

We entered and found only one other couple there at the end of the bar. It was about 10 p.m., so it was almost closing time. We went to the other end of the bar to give them privacy, as they were deep in conversation.

Just as we got our glasses of wine, I heard the woman laugh. *I knew that laugh*! The whole time I

was in Carmel I'd been hoping I
might come upon someone from my
past to be comfortable with. I
walked over and introduced myself.
She didn't recognize me after
thirty years, but when she finally
did, her first comment was:
"Aren't you that wise guy, beach
bum, I knew in college?" I
acknowledged that I was. She
invited me and my sister to join
her and her brother. She'd gone by
a nickname; now, however, I was
somehow inspired to call her by
her middle name, Annie. When my
sister met Annie's brother, it was
love at first sight. They were
married two months later. But
that's another story.

Annie has been my partner,
first mate, and best friend for
the past 17 years. *The Father of
the Forest had heard my plea!*

I was looking for a sailboat.
I had lost my beautiful
*Patronilla,* a Rhodes-designed
plank cutter sailboat, in the ugly
divorce. I had nowhere to live.

Displaced from my sister's
home after she met Annie's
brother, he and I simply changed
places, and I now stayed with

Annie! We started traveling,
looking for a design sailboat that
would take us around the world.
The fiberglass Columbia 50 with
old-world lines caught my eye. It
was the first fiberglass boat of
its size ever built, and there
were doubts about how it would
survive. William Tripp used the
best hull design and sail
configuration to balance the boat
perfectly.

It had a formidable
reputation for being a fast
passage maker and bringing one
home safely. We looked and looked,
as there were only a few built.
Finally, I found one in terrible
condition that I could afford to
pay cash for. It took all my
resources, but I had found work
running a tugboat for the same
bridge company I worked for
before. I couldn't stand being in
debt again, so I paid cash.

So began our life aboard, and
here we still are, six thousand
miles later. Up and down the
California Coast we went, from the
Bay Area to around the Coronado
Islands in Mexico. It was an epic
retrofit, a true test for man and

woman. Now, after almost seventeen years, our boat is still going strong.

The early passing of my mother and my share of her estate had made this abundance possible. We had a home! And all this, right out of my pocket! What a great new beginning for me! Deficit spending had really cost me. When I found out, during my divorce proceedings, how deeply in debt we were due to our overuse of credit cards, I vowed, *No more!*

After six years of enjoying the sailing on San Pablo Bay and the greater San Francisco Bay, I was getting frustrated with car traffic. It was thirty minutes to get to work on the San Mateo Bridge, and two and a half hours, stuck in traffic, to get back to Alameda, where we were moored at the time.

With an ocean-sailing vessel, I was eager to feel the swell under my keel, and watch the California Coast sliding by us as we caught the trade winds down the coast. I had a decent job but simply got, what I felt, "squeezed out." Besides, I was anxious to

see how *Allure* -- we renamed her
to give her a brighter future than
what she had been through -- would
feel on the open sea.

We had worked our way down
the coast from the Bay Area to
Monterey, Ventura, Whittier, and
San Diego, all one year apart. I
liked leaving an old harbor and
enjoyed entering a new one.

As a crane operator and with a
captain's license, I could find
work anywhere on the coast
operating the Tug and then running
a crane on the barge I was
pushing. The problem was finding a
place to live. The marinas were
filling up with people who
couldn't afford a house or even an
apartment. So when I would call
about a potential slip for the
boat, the marina owner would
automatically say, "No live-on-
boards!" I learned to suggest
that I was working for the state,
and offered to pay three months in
advance. This usually got us a
place.

We'd gone to San Diego with
expectations of moving on to
Mexico and Central America. San
Diego is truly the place with all

the amenities for a cruising
sailboat. There was no room in any
of the marinas in San Diego, but
in the end, it worked out better
by far. We found a delightful
marina in Chula Vista. Twelve
miles south of San Diego on a
channel, they welcomed us with
open arms. However, we did have to
sail twelve miles up the channel
just to get to San Diego.

Now I see why they had room
for us; very few people wanted to
be that far away from the downtown
area. We could see Mexico from our
slip. I was able to sit in on a
calypso band in a local
restaurant, Bob's on the Bay. I
played a set of congas and was
thoroughly enjoying my time there;
however, walking through the bar
on the way to the boat was taking
its toll on my trim figure. I was
working as a crane operator on a
barge, doing the seismic retrofit
of the Coronado Bridge at the
time. Life was good.

But then Annie was suddenly
called to care for her elderly
parents, so we had to make a
decision. Either we'd split up and
go our separate ways, or I'd find

another shipmate, or we'd join forces in responding to Annie's situation and move back up the coast. There was no question for me.

Annie had been through the worst. I thought about her having to climb over the relocated engine, in the middle of the passageway, to get to our bunk in the fos'cle (forward sleeping area). I thought about her dealings with the "head" (marine toilet), which had become a putrid mess we from previous owners that had leaked under the floorboards. She diligently cleaned the mess up, and I rebuilt the head. Above all, Annie was the woman I had asked Father Forest to find for me, and I'd certainly not abandon her in her time of need.

We sailed up the coast back to Ventura, where she could commute to her parents' house. It was on this passage that I had the epiphany that I wanted to collect quartz crystals and study their metaphysical properties.

Water flying in our faces, seemingly square seas, and our bird "Spanky" all of a sudden

speaking out! "Hold 'er to it!"
(This refers to holding coarse of
the vessel no matter what). We'd
taught him to say that, and he
only used it when the going got so
rough that he had to hold on to
his cage with his beak! This was
an inside joke with us and always
caused us to laugh no matter how
fearful we became. Spanky was a
true source of entertainment for
us.

Spanky would freak out if I
left the cockpit while Annie was
below, and the vessel, under sail
and on autopilot; she slid
gracefully through the water
unattended. He didn't like to be
left alone at sea. He would "go
off" with loud chirping, which
would bring Annie up with some
loud chirping of her own! She
never liked my leaving the cockpit
as I could have fallen overboard!
I caught hell whenever Spanky
"busted me."

So, with due ceremony, we
promoted Spanky from "Swabby" to
"Mate," as he was pulling his
weight as our new watch-bird.. We
had champagne while Spanky enjoyed

his "tot of sake," which was his
favorite.

IT'S ABOUT COMPASSION

Chapter 15

We'd been living in Ventura now
for seven years. Our lives had
taken an interesting turn -- by
fate, I suppose. We grew to love
this little oasis between Santa
Barbara, the crowded Simi Valley,
and greater Los Angeles. Eighteen
miles off the coast is an island
group called the Channel Islands,
a national park with no amenities
compared to Catalina Island.

Catalina is so crowded off the
coast of Long Beach that you have
to check in and pay for a mooring
to secure your boat. Not so in the

Channel Islands group. With rocky bottom in many places and irregular "sundowner" winds blowing at sunset down canyons on Santa Cruz Island, it would be calm one minute and then blowing 50 knots from the opposite direction. You had to be cautious about it, but everyone seemed used to it, as it lasted only about two hours.

We loved it, as it gave us a destination to sail to and go fishing. A three-hour sail and we were on our own, often all alone and gently swinging to the anchor. We enjoyed our life on board.

This is about the time when I happened to go to Carmel to visit my sister. And then one day I met a crystal skull on a back shelf and my life changed forever.

Chronicling the experiences of others with this skull sets me apart from most mainstream caretakers, who make up some of the most creative stories about the origins of their skulls. One such story holds that some skulls were carved from a larger one that happened to be ancient, therefore making the knock-off skulls ancient also. Go figure.

I feel it is up to my guests to paint the picture of who this skull is, by reporting what it did for them personally. The combination of their testimony goes a long way toward defining just who this crystal skull is. I like to live with a clear conscience, and frankly, I am not cunning enough to perpetuate a lie for long. I would be catching myself up in such a lie, as you will see that many others have, if you research their claims.

The crystal skulls that are working to heal or educate the community of man have my deepest respect. I hope to see Compassion listed among them when she becomes better known for what she does instead of what she could possibly be.

I did not ask for this experience with a crystal skull, as I keep saying, but am grateful that the path my life has taken enables me to be of service by sharing Compassion, and telling others about the Sacred Feminine energies that she represents as

many have told me. And never fear:
They are coming not by the much
heralded deadline of December 21,
2012, but rather as an ongoing
process of continual shifting in
consciousness. If there is to be
destruction and loss of life, so
be it, those will be prepared for
the ascension. This is a much
higher path than I could ever have
imagined, and very unexpected for
someone with my background. I am
learning that this is just the
beginning of a consciousness
revolution so sorely needed for
thousands of years.

Since she has come into my
life, I have spent most of my time
with Compassion right next to me.
This has allowed me to gaze at her
and talk to her as one does with a
friend. The sun brings rainbows to
her face, and the full moon
creates an indescribably different
appearance in her. Resting my hand
on Compassion -- which I very
seldom do -- I have gotten an
overwhelming feeling of
unconditional Love. **(Fig.6)**

I'd asked people at the skull
conference in Tempe to write to us
describing their experiences with

Compassion. Annie and I were so high from the experience of meeting all those wonderful and sensitive people that it's a wonder we had the presence of mind to ask for their input! I felt it important to chronicle the events, maybe for some future needs which I am unaware of today.

One such sensitive person is Ziranna. She'd come up to our table to ask if she could sit with Compassion and us. In her hands was the most beautiful smoky quartz skull one could ever imagine. We got her a chair and made her comfortable, as she was having difficulty breathing and walking, and was very weak. Ziranna's shortness of breath and tentative movements reminded me of when my own knees were bone on bone.

In subsequent correspondence she told us the powerful embrace of Compassion had overcome her; she was breathless from exertion I suppose. This is what she wrote;

"*Joseph, it helped me a lot to be able to sit by you both. I feel that someday we will have a purpose together, probably with many others. There was so much going on at an energy level at the conference; I know you got the information and the clearing that was appropriate. It is important to be as clear as possible when working with the beautiful energies. Your skull is very, very powerful.*

*I felt privileged to spend time with her. I recognized her; I have worked with her at some point in my evolution, maybe on Atlantis, as that seems to be when I worked with crystals a lot. Some of the information has surfaced, and some has not yet. This is a powerful time to be on Earth, and we have chosen to be here.*

*I am waking up to my purpose of working with the skulls; many other of my areas have opened but that one is still opening. With my connection with the Cosmic Mother, this has helped me a lot. You can't have a closed heart and work with her energies. Love and light, Ziranna"*

This woman was quite frail, possibly in her late sixties. She was wearing beautiful flowing robes and carrying the aforementioned unusual crystal skull, with much golden Angel hair rutile. There were over two hundred people there, and of all of them, this woman was sensitive enough to act on her need to be with Compassion.

She said she wanted to be healed by Compassion's Energy. This was new to me. I know some caretakers have made claims of healing, but have never seen any healing myself. After she had been with us for a while she calmed down, started breathing easily, and told us a little about herself. But most of her attention went to Compassion and the people who were drawn to her.

The people came and went, some leaving their skulls for us to watch as they wandered off to see the display tables. Some asked whether we had "skulls for sale" that were "energized" by Compassion's presence.

"No," I said. "We just came here to share our crystal skull Compassion." This got some funny looks, as if they felt obligated to make a purchase. I couldn't imagine leaving expensive skulls and walking away to shop, especially considering that they already had a couple of crystal skulls.

"Sure." We just said we watch them leaving their expensive crystal skulls, and off they would go. This helped me understand the underlying motive of the skull conference. It was not for us.

With many testimonials, I loaded my website. I won't go into them here, but suffice it to say that women are very drawn to Compassion. Men who are in touch with their creative sides are also touched by her presence. She seems to be a vehicle to take people places and, for some, a means of opening energy points in themselves. She is definitely becoming known as the symbol of the Sacred Feminine.

Three times during sessions people have had to either leave the area for a while, or return to the area. Some felt their crown chakra open up with a bang. Some felt their heart chakra opening. They all thanked me for the experience. Others, who were not prepared, were just plain frightened.

I warn people now to expect some feelings along their body's energy meridians. What I get personally is not important at this time; suffice it to say that I get some real physical shocks.

In May of the following year, I was invited to a Meet-up group in San Diego led by a shaman-trained man named David Shadowolf. He has spent much time in Guatemala and Mexico with the medicine people. He and his beautiful wife Caroline are the parents of a little girl named Maia. They invited me down for a "Healing the Waters of the Gulf" prayer vigil after the oil spill.

He didn't know of my experience with the oil spill in Alaska, but had seen pictures of Compassion and was happy to read that I was doing presentations with such a unique skull for no fee.

David had several skulls of his own and had sold some. Like me, he was disillusioned with how the whole crystal skull phenomenon was being "spun" into the very thing

the skulls have been telling us to
move away from. He didn't pass any
judgments; he just stuck to his
path, loving everyone.

I went alone; Annie and
Phyllis couldn't make it. It was
another long trip  -- LA driving
has to be timed just so to get
through it without too much
congestion. Annie and I used to
live there in 2001. I was
operating a freeway-grinding
machine at the time, cutting
concrete to smooth out the bumps.

David and Caroline were kind
enough to put me up, thus saving
me motel fees. Theirs is a very
interesting stucco home with a
flat, Mexican-style roof that I
really admired. I especially
enjoyed the relaxed atmosphere and
the short walk to almost
everything one needs -- including
what I in particular needed, which
was a great, authentic Mexican
restaurant.

Caroline was a gracious
hostess, moving gracefully around
--  a baby on her hip - to attend
to her guest.  Their love was
palpable as they welcomed
Compassion and me with open arms.

What David wanted to do is use an established amphitheater to take advantage of its semicircular shape and fire pit in the center. He'd place his skulls on the seats to raise them from the sand, with Compassion and her Lemurians in the center. We were right on the edge of Mission Bay.

To showcase Compassion and the other crystals, and give everybody a good time, David paid for and organized a volunteer free meal at the amphitheater. It was great; we had about forty people come and go. The interesting aspect to me was the passersby just walking the beach. I saw a group of Latinos who were all dressed up, enjoying the park while walking past the skull display, after church I assume. They appeared to be drawn to the skulls, stopped, looked at each other, bewildered, and walked away. I didn't try to engage them as I respected their privacy.

With all the Lemurian crystals I had brought for the occasion, I wanted to create an Earth Healing Grid. We had a great time setting it up, and ten straight hours of enjoying the skulls. Free to the public, everyone had a chance to come and experience the skulls. We had bikers, homeless people, businesspeople, park rangers. No boundaries or fences.

David and Caroline Shadowolf are truly a blessing to humanity. Caroline is also an aeronautical engineer, and is from a Spanish family in Guatemala that has set up schools for underprivileged young girls.

"They never get a chance for an education," Caroline told me. She and her family are giving back in a big way; they're not only providing for the schools financially, but also offering their time and energy. These are very beautiful people who are living a life of "Compassion." Not an easy thing to do, as we all know.

David was keen on making a video of himself meditating with Compassion. He would go into trance and recount what he saw while in a deep meditative state. This worked out well, but the sound was all but not there with

this camera. David later added his
words to the film, and they were
most informative. Though original
and sincere, David is like me in
that he does not have a literary
background; his calling is to
gather people and share the love
that is in his heart. He and his
family will be with me always, as
they are living in compassion.

KATHERINE'S SESSIONS

Chapter 16

Upon my return from David and
Caroline's, I called Katherine
Rosengren to see how she was
doing. We had shared her backyard

for the first invitational viewing of Compassion.

I wanted to speak with her about her abilities. After working for many years in hospice care, she had become increasingly sensitive to spirits, and was able to communicate with them due to her work with a close friend that works with Spirits.

She asked whether I thought Compassion would be suitable for this, as she'd noticed her sending a blue ray straight up during our meditations. I didn't know but agreed to come over and see what would happen.

It was July when I visited. I had Compassion with me, and Katherine and I chatted for a while. We like to tease each other about being dyslexic, which causes much laughter between us. Eventually settling down, we started to meditate with Compassion between us on a coffee table in her living room. The following is the actual process that Katherine went through to conduct the sessions we would undertake later. But first, a little about her background.

Working as an active hospice RN, Katherine was Director and Trainer of Hospice Volunteers and Director of Hospice Bereavement Services at the Santa Clara Home Support Group and. She is a facilitator for a variety of hospice and other support groups for people of all ages, including Alzheimer's caregiver support groups in the tri-county area. In addition, she teaches several online courses in "Conscious Death and Dying" for a certificate program in thanatology, with Cue's for professionals available.

Katherine's academic credentials include an RN in the State of California, a B.A. in psychology, and a master's degree in transpersonal psychology.

She is an ordained minister and Reiki Master who has trained and extensively studied with shamans in Native American traditions and other cultures around the world.

She holds "The Divine Healing Grant" (Osazukay) bestowed only in Tenrikyo, Japan, where she studied and was granted this sacred honor. Katherine is a published poet, an artist, and a teacher of meditation.

Here is Katherine's story:

*"I met Joseph and Compassion in July 2009, and at the time, I had a strong sense that she, Compassion, was linked in some way to helping others make their transition into the Light. This would of course be in addition to whatever else the consciousness anchored within the crystal skull we call Compassion may be destined to do.*

*After several months of establishing a solid working relationship with them both, I began having dreams about working with Joe and Compassion. In meditations, it became clear that we should proceed, ultimately adding more people when the time seems right.*

*I waited for some confirmation in the Light before agreeing to participate in this kind of meditation with Joseph and Compassion.*

*Whenever I am joining any new group with a set intention, it is important for me to sense a guidance and a calling that this is the correct action to take for the Highest Good. Having done this work on a continuous basis since 9/11, and following major natural catastrophes, it is obvious that there is a need among souls who, for whatever reason, have not yet gone into the Light.*

*Many are not yet aware that they no longer function in a physical body. Some of these souls have chosen -- possibly erroneously -- to remain "behind" for their loved ones. People in groups that have met a sudden and unexpected end to physical life may be similarly motivated. There are many reasons, but these are the most common." -- Katherine Rosengren*

*At the beginning of our first session, Katherine would smudge the room with sage and do her own ceremony. When I was seated, she would ask that guardian archangels come down and protect us while opening a "path of Light" for lost souls to follow to higher realms. There was more, but it is unnecessary for this story.*

*I asked that she speak aloud, so I could follow her work. Below are her words as the first session unfolded. I have her permission to use this information as we are still doing sessions together. I feel this is very important work we are doing with Compassion, and illustrates one of the many facets of this crystal skull.*

*"Session One: March 5th, 2010. Helping those in need to travel onward into the light.*

*Present: Joe Bennett, the Crystal Skull Compassion, Katherine Rosengren, and Beings of Life and Light, both seen and unseen, offering their assistance and protection.*

*Preparations: Very little. Basically, the room or space we work in is smudged and cleared, as are we and Compassion, creating a safe and sacred space. Compassion seems to serve as a beacon for earthbound souls while also enhancing our personal awareness of those seeking help.*

*Joseph had not done this work before, so I talked us through it out loud. This method seemed to work for us, and we are continuing in this vein to this day.*

Interesting things, new to me, occurred. Perhaps that's because Joseph is a retired Alaskan fisherman, has built and lived in log cabins in Alaska, and traveled extensively. He has picked up survival and life skills that members of the prior groups had lacked. And of course, Compassion, a Keeper of the Sacred Feminine and Its Lineage, was also a novel addition for me.

First, a little girl I had seen for several years came to us. I kept seeing her, over the years, then dreamt of her twice in the prior week. She seemed very at ease with us and eager to pass onward into the Light. She came immediately, fascinated by Compassion, and then went into the Light with ease. But then (a first for me) she returned a while later to remain with us. She knelt beside Compassion, who was placed on a low table between Joe and me, until we closed the meditation about an hour later.

Those still waiting were sent onward to other helpful groups around the world. I explained that the Light is always available, if *they just ask, and that we may be doing this again soon in the same way and at the same place.*

*Next came a few ragtag families, but mostly men from the Dust Bowl area of the Midwestern plains. These were farmers who seemed to have tried hard to save their families, but had "gotten lost" in the focus of their own deep grief. They'd become confused about how to go on. Some seemed to be waiting in case their families returned home to them. Then, hardhat-wearing miners lined up from what appeared to be a coal mine in the southern United States or somewhere in the east. All were wearing boots and carrying picks or lunchboxes.*

*Some were very angry, some exhausted, and many were riddled with guilt -- perhaps from an accident, murder, or inability to get the others out. A few seemed to be in charge of making sure the others got out safely. In their panic and fear, all had missed the natural order of going into the Light...and had been left to wait for help to find them.*

I debriefed the men,
explaining that they no longer
needed to stay there, and pointed
out that they were no longer in
need of the physical bodies they
saw themselves in. The men would
watch Joseph as I directed them to
the Light. His big, solid yet
loving presence seemed to reassure
them that they were doing the
right thing for themselves and
their crews.

I suggested that they look up
and watch for an angel or family
member who would be waiting for
them in the Light, and reassured
them that someone always comes to
greet the newcomers. Many looked
at Compassion with curiosity.

There was a strong sense that
Compassion was functioning as a
beacon, and that Joe's working
blue-collar energy resonated with
some of the men who had been
stuck. Like Joe's, theirs was a
strong work loyalty ethic, and
they did not want to leave their
families or co-workers behind.

Again, some were initially
very angry. They were able to
release that anger, transmuting it
into Light and then, as if a great

*weight had been lifted from their shoulders, they went into the Light…*

*Then villagers arrived from South America or Mesoamerica, possibly Mayans. One man didn't want to let go of his burro; another refused to leave his two dozen chickens until they had a person they trusted to "keep them." It seemed as if an earthquake or volcano had taken them all out fast.*

*After explaining why they no longer needed their bodies, it occurred to me that they were Catholic. This was around the same time I became aware of "the Lady in White," who'd come to an open portal with outstretched arms.*

*They hesitated until I was guided to assure them that the animals would be safe in Joseph's keeping. The first man in line handed Joe the rope to his burro, and the man with the chickens kept a close eye on Joe as he shooed them over beside him. Who'd given them a nod of reassurance? After the first few felt safe, the entire village of men, women, and children followed quickly.*

*We were able to work well in tandem, since I was speaking what I sensed aloud, and Joe could respond intuitively. Again, there was a brief hiatus as Compassion seemed to suddenly send out a strong focus of golden light.*

*Our next set of visitors was an ancient group that seemed to see a deity I was unfamiliar with. One of the leaders of the villages went "onward into the Light." Then whole streams of people followed – a veritable blur of discarnate spirits. Evidently, they'd been waiting for "permission" to go onward.*

*Almost immediately, a group of men in a South American crystal mine began to climb up out of the depths and toward the sunlight. Some were angry with the owners up on top whom they had worked and died for. Others appeared relieved, as they emerged slowly from the depths.*

*Below them, I sensed a pool of water... in which were skeletons...I began to invite them out of the deep pool in the bottom of the cave and was stopped. We*

*were well protected from the other
side. (higher dimensions)*

*I asked that Beings of Light go
down and help prepare them to move
on to wherever they needed to go
next. There are times, though,
when caution and free will both
need to be honored to maintain
safety and ethical standards. If a
soul is not supposed to go into
the Light, that becomes clear very
fast. Those meditations are left
for another time and place."*

The above account is accurate
and a direct quote from dear
Katherine Rosengren. During this
experience, there were times when
I felt strong emotions, but I did
not see any spirits myself. We had
three more sessions after this
that may be seen on the website.
Katherine volunteers all the
information. I ask her to
chronicle the events.

During one of our later
sessions, Katherine got very
drained doing this work and needed
to take a break. We were in a deep
meditation and about finished when
I had my first vision.

"Say, Katherine, I see a boat
with four people who just came

into the room." (It was chest level to me) Her answer startled me.

"How many are there, and how old?" I felt that I would lose the vision if I looked directly at it, but followed her lead.

"Four people -- two adults and two adolescents, all standing up in the boat that has stopped right next to me. They are looking down at Compassion."

Not missing a beat, Katherine asked them to please disembark from the boat. She informed them that they were deceased now, and that the boat was only an illusion they were hanging on to.

After they reluctantly departed the boat, Katherine directed them to the Light. She said they were no longer lost and were just where they needed to be to pass on.

"You can go into the Light now," she said in a reassuringly soft tone, and they instantly flashed past her. While I didn't see this part of the experience, I was happy I was finally able to see, in my mind's eye, some earthbound spirits. Just then, a

golden retriever appeared next to
my head on my right side. All I
could see was his head and neck
from the corner of my eye.
"I have a dog next to me, what do
we do?" I stammered.

Surprised, Katherine
responded, "I have never helped an
animal pass through to the Light."
She was even more surprised when a
smaller light opened up at floor
level, and the dog dashed right
for it! She said.

She was very excited and
relieved, as this set a precedent
for her. It was certainly a shock
for me to hear, as once again, I
had not been able to see that
part.

My role is only to
demonstrate that we have the
capacity to see more than we give
ourselves credit for, or more than
we wish to believe. So this is the
way things are still going, and
why I say Compassion is a "working
skull."

Annie feels that this one of
the most important thing
Compassion is doing now, and might
be what she does after the "Great
Shift." She has not been present

at a session, but wants to hear all about it when I return home. She feels this work is for Katherine and me only.

Annie relates this to others, as she is now working with people who have lost loved ones, or are about to. Her principal resource in this work is a wonderful book, *Dying into Freedom,* by thanatology's Susan C. Storch, RN, MA.

Annie's mother has her own collection of crystals. She makes her own grids, which I think is just brilliant. Her mind is sharp and does not miss a thing. We have sat and talked for hours about many subjects, and argued about a few. I have very much respect for this lady. Our sessions continue as connect finding the time to sit with Compassion. Last session, December 2011, Annie ask to join us. Usually it's just Katherine, Compassion and myself. We took our respective places after Katherine smudged the room and us as we entered. She said there were Spirits waiting in her hall way to "come in."

I didn't see any Spirits on this occasion as it's been a while since we sat together. Annie said she saw Compassion with golden "rods" shooting out of her skull. Then a "Blue Cloud" enveloped Annie in her minds eye and traveled to and encompassed Compassion she told us. This is a first and I hope when Annie joins us next time she will open up to see more.

Katherine has writing up our experience so out of respect for her work I will post it on my web site for those that would like to follow this work. We are awaiting our next session as everyone has to find the time and be relaxed

COMPASSION AT NO CHARGE

Chapter 17

Annie and I had met some people in a tiny Arizona town called Yarnell. It was along our way to Tempe, where we'd attended the 9/9/9 World Mysteries Conference. It's up in the high desert, about four thousand feet. We still didn't have any air conditioning. I offered to get it fixed, I truly wanted Annie to come with me.

"We can use the squirt bottles again," she said, which suggested to me that she was up for going. She knew it would be expensive and has always been a "Team Player." But first she had to make some changes in the care of her mother. She has an

overnight person who trades off
with Annie during the week.

He is young, and Annie's mom
is ninety-five. He is also a
professional drummer, who is
giving her lessons with his whole
drum setup in her living room. I
think it's terrific. He takes her
out to lunch, and she has a
strong, caring young man to take
her arm. She was married to the
same man for seventy years. He
passed the day my granddaughter
was born.

So there we were again,
rolling along in the sweltering
heat, bound for Yarnell, Arizona.
As mariners, the desert holds some
fascination for us. Endless
expanses of rolling hills with
sagebrush and barbed-wire fences.
To us "coasties," who enjoy the
refreshing breezes coming off the
sea every day, it felt like
driving into a blast furnace.
Annie would spray my legs, the
back of my neck, and my arms with
ice water!

"YEOOOW!" I yelled when I
didn't see it coming -- quite a
shock. We drove through little
dust-blown towns along Interstate

10, gradually entering the vast desert. Nothing for miles in every direction. A road that was well maintained and so straight it was easy to lose focus and drift off into a "heat-treated daydream."

I would have done just that but for Annie's diligent ice water blast. Hour after hour, we were driving at seventy miles per hour, yet it seemed like we were holding up traffic when he hit Arizona. The people were driving like maniacs! I would guess the average speed was around ninety miles per hour.

Speaking to a waitress when we stopped for something to eat, I began to understand. The residents of Arizona had wanted to change the speed limit to ninety, but it was not approved. Talk about insane! In this heat, you have to be especially alert -- anything running across the highway would be struck as soon as you saw it! If one car had a problem, the ones behind it would smash into the car ahead of them so fast they wouldn't know what hit them. This made Annie extremely nervous.

"Compassion is traveling with us, and would not allow anything to interfere with her agenda, Annie," I tried to console her.

"Well, just tell those speed freaks that!" Boy, it certainly made us feel our age as we poked along. Then, in a flash (blur!), I saw people older than we flying by, as if they were trying to take off and fly!

I guess people like us just get used to it; we just moved over a bit to signal, "We're *trying* to get out of your way!"
I was more sensitive to the one-hundred-twelve-degree heat blowing into my window. We started to climb into the mountains. Temperatures cooled off, and the traffic had to slow down. It was now about 80 degrees, and refreshing. I realized then that I love the high desert; its air felt clear, and my arthritis didn't hurt quite so badly.

We reached the top of the mountain range to rediscover the little residential communities along the way to Prescott, Arizona. Yarnell is tiny, with a history of gold and silver mining.

It was auspicious, considering that on our first trip through here I was in a hurry to get to air conditioning, and cool drinks.

Annie was telling me to enjoy the scenery. Good advice, as all of a sudden a massive pyramid loomed before me on the left side of the road about 40 feet tall! I slammed on the brakes. What I was seeing were roughly 55° angles just like the ones in Mexico I had seen on the History Channel's "Ancient Aliens." series.

"Look Annie, look!" I was calling out, but Annie was distracted. Right across the opposite side of the street from the pyramid was a house with Hopi rugs and blankets of all colors, hung up and flapping in the light breeze. It looked like a cross between a carpet shop and a yard sale. We backed up and pulled in, then met the man living there.

Ed was a raku potter who had the most colorful display of hand-thrown lamps, vases, bowls, and plates that I'd ever seen. The colors were vibrant. I learned that the raku process brings out

the colors, but at a price. Most
of the pieces are broken in the
kiln that is buried in the ground.

I spotted a large vase I
would love to have owned, but
couldn't afford, as we were on a
tight travel budget. Besides, this
was hardly the time for me to shop
for pottery! However, these were
some of the finest works of art I
had ever seen. This fascinating
man lived his art, spending most
his time alone, his hands deep in
clay.

What we were both particularly
drawn to was his large Zen garden.
Enclosed by a fence and some shade
trees, it was filled with washed
pea gravel, large volcanic rocks,
statues, and fountains, all with
lighting. Cascading water in the
desert made for such a soothing
contrast.

Annie and I agreed that we
had to go back someday and visit
him after meeting him the first
time on our way through to Tempe.

Annie said she wanted to give
me the raku vase I liked so much,
with the Hopi katsina doll on the
front. It was all about the desert
coloring of the Southwest. I loved

it, but could not justify buying a lovely vase simply for boat décor!

Now as we were speaking with Ed, his wife Darlene called to ask whether she could invite some people over to meet us. We'd gotten into a discussion concerning some quartz crystals the last time we were together in Yarnell. Darlene and others in her group were metaphysical friends were talking about the properties of quartz crystals.

I overheard that conversation, and asked Annie to see if they knew anything about the prophecy of the thirteen crystal skulls.

Annie handed me the phone. Darlene told me they were indeed informed and would invite still more friends in their little town who might be interested in a Full Moon Ceremony with Lunar Eclipse, which happened to fall on my birthday.

So now I had an impromptu event. Making it free to the public makes it easier to do that. We did stop, for old times' sake, and have a late lunch to get out of the heat. When we got to

Yarnell, it was June, 2010 just
about dusk. I wanted to check out
that pyramid I'd glimpsed earlier
across the street.

Ed the potter, who lived
across the street from it, had
told me that it showed magnetic
disturbances picked up by the
surveyors. In addition, it was
composed of granite boulders. They
weren't stacked but appeared to
have been dropped after something
lifted them up and then let it all
just rain down, like a handful of
sand. As any builder of
sandcastles knows, this forms a
pyramid shape.

However, these boulders were
several hundred pounds each; the
pyramid had to be forth feet tall
and three hundred feet in
circumference.

I noticed some small guest
cabins around the area, and a
sprinkling of trees. William told
me there was a stream that ran
along its base but didn't know if
it ran all year long.

Our hosts were happy to see
us, asked about our trip, and
suggested we check into the B & B

just down the street  before we
started our ceremony.

This was an excellent idea,
as it was still light out, and we
could freshen up before the event
started. When we returned, we
found that Darlene had created a
place with an outside table where
she said the moon shone most
brightly when it crested the hill
from the east.

I placed Compassion on her
turntable to catch the last rays
of the sun after she'd been in her
dark carrying case. She lit right
up, and I was happy. I carefully
placed the ten-pound Lemurians at
all four cardinal points, asking
them to create a protective grid
around Compassion. I declined the
offer, but I could see that
everyone who was coming was
accustomed to sharing the host's
wine at her get-togethers. (I
guess I just have to adapt. In
retrospect, it occurs to me that
most of the people had come just
to marvel at the uniqueness of the
crystal skull.)

The sun was setting over what
I have come to call the Pyramid in
the West. The large crystals and

Compassion took this lower-angle light and reflected it back to the people attending. It was rather sad to see the sun leave, as backlighted with her sentinels, Compassion had been very beautiful. I greeted the assembled group.

"Thank you all for coming. I know this was impromptu, and that some of you know little about the crystal skulls that are making themselves known at this time in our history." I got a thank you from the group.

"The practice of capitalism is our way now. However, many are disillusioned not only by materialism but also by organized religion who's edicts are being overturned by science, and a science that turns its back on the myths and legends of the ancients. Perhaps more than ever before, people need to feel their personal connection to God - a union that is not conditional. I feel that this pretty much sums up the situation that science and technologies are putting us in today.

"I read somewhere that 'science gives us words we can't pronounce, and measures life with a bathroom scale and ruler. It takes away the mystery that makes it all mean something.' Gathering as we are now to discuss this topic, is another part of what the skulls have come back for, in my opinion."

I explained what I felt and had gleaned from my reading about the purpose of the crystal skulls in our world at this time. I also touched upon the Mayan prophecy and the Mayan calendar, along with creation myths and the possibility of having been visited by extraterrestrials before recorded history. Some believe that E.T.s built or supervised the building of great pyramids, various massive structures that mainstream scientists cannot explain. Our so-called "advanced" technology could not replicate many things found to be from an long ago ancient age that built from stone to survive the type of coming cataclysm told about in so many cultures....

I discussed how basic quartz has given us our Electronic Age, noting the piezoelectric capabilities of quartz and how iron oxide is the magnetic connection.

Following a Q & A session, I had each guest place a crystalline being alongside Compassion to upload information, as some say. Then we were through for the evening, as it was getting cold.

After a final prayer, the people thanked us for coming so far to their little community and wished us a safe drive home. Annie and I saw this informal and improvised meeting as confirmation of people's willingness to nurture one another with love.

It has been pointed out to us that Compassion may be perceived as the spirit of Mary Magdalene or Quan Yin, according to one's belief system. But for the Buddhist, the Hindu, the Cathar Christian, or any sincere seeker, no matter what she is called, there is one common description of her, and that is COMPASSION. Compassion as empathy and caring for one another, Compassion for the trees, the grass, the water and the air we breathe. It is a

way of looking at and responding
to life that is the hallmark of
the changes that are coming on
December 21, 2012.

No one knows what to expect
except things will be changing in
the evolution of Man and Earth.
It's nothing less than a spiritual
renaissance for mankind. Some
people are grasping it and have
dropped out, or are no longer
attached to the system. Ours is a
world of false security, offering
endless distraction while using up
natural resources for our
privileged few of us.

While this is not entirely
our fault, we can now see that
passive trust in our leaders to
consider the plight of the rest of
the world has been naively
misplaced or ignored. I am told
have moved to a very low and heavy
vibration of self-gratification,
greed, and hunger for power over
others at the expense of all that
really matters, including our
home, Mother Earth. We all will be
on the same playing field of an
agromic society they say. We are
about to learn the hard way that
we are only "guests" on this

beautiful Garden of Eden planet we call Earth. The transition will be difficult for many. Compassion's eyes appear so sad. They say she has seen it all before in Atlantis.

It has been said by the sensitives in ancient Mexico, Guatemala brought forth in our time that singing crystal skulls were there in Atlantis, urging people to try to see a larger picture than their own selfish gratification.

Mayan legends tell of "Singing Crystal Skulls," hand-carved with the information of other worlds held inside until mankind finds the proper frequency to unlock this information.

Bringing Compassion with the concept of compassion to the people is likely to offer valuable benefits. For one thing, it inspires confidence, letting people know they can be free even in a densely populated city. We can all learn to respect the Earth that can give us everything we need. We learn to provide for ourselves, gardening on rooftops, learn to work together with mutual respect. It is the next logical move to get out of the crowded metropolitan areas and into the country.

People across America are already doing it. Their perception of money can shift from being a major focus to an incidental one, leading to the ethos of depending on one another for basic needs, as my wife and I did in Alaska.

This Garden of Eden, a place of so many diverse and beautiful life forms, can grow and prosper. A thought of compassion goes out into the cosmos. The thought takes form and becomes reality on a subtler plane of existence, finally manifesting right here in our material world. Also, I am optimistic about finding the proper vibration to unlock the singing crystal skulls. Whoever has the tone, the right sound, could light up the skulls and make them sing with the wisdom of long ago and far away -- or even other planes of existence close to, or interpenetrating, our own. These songs may well include answers to our Big Questions of illness, famine, war, pestilence, and even

death. We have been given a tool
that we may use, both now and
after the 2012 awakening and shift
in consciousness, enabling us to
help those who didn't "get it." A
place to meditate and look into
the stars, Compassions eyes, as
you can all doing now, finding
your own frequency to bring you
up, to that which you really are,
Children of the Universe.

We ended our visit in Yarnell
and traveled back to our "good old
boat." Now I am arranging free
sessions with the Crystal Skull
Compassion through groups, in
hopes of getting her message out
and ever looking for the right
frequency to enable her to speak
and sing! Not being a media person
and having to tell the truth about
Compassion means to me I have to
have confidence Compassion will
call to those that reaching out to
her.

OUT OF AFRICA

Chapter 18


In 2010, I contacted the well-
known investigative journalist
Philip Coppens. He returned my

email after seeing the photos of
Compassion that I sent him. I had
seen his work on the History
Channel's "Ancient Aliens." It is
grounded and they expresses their
opinions.

Because he lived within 100
miles, I invited him to come here
to examine Compassion for himself.
Philip was amazed by her
proportions, and especially the
iron oxide encapsulated in her
cranium. I told him my history
with the skull and how I was at
first unwilling to become the
caretaker.

I wondered: Could Philip
suggest a way to get Compassion's
story out to the world? He told me
Compassion was doing just fine,
and would "come out" at her own
speed.

When the day arrived we drove
the distance into the Los Angeles
area and found their home to be
particularly spacious after coming
from a sailboat. All of their
guests warmly welcomed us.

I set Compassion down on the
living room table; although we're
not in the habit of leaving
Compassion out of our sight, the

feel of this home was far from
threatening. We noticed that the
Abyssinian cat had made a beeline
for Compassion and was now curled
up with her. It was as if this
mystical Egyptian cat – some
believe of royal ancestry -- had
come to guard, or simply be close
to Compassion. When we all went
into the adjoining room, we found
it strange that the cat would not
budge. Evidently, this was her
spot.

Philip was particularly
interested in Compassion's life in
Africa, and wanted to know whether
she  could be traced to Egypt. I
had to say no, because the
salesman was curiously guarded
about the man whom he bought her
from.

The only thing I could tell
him for sure was that the man who
sold him the skull returned to
Africa. Then it sat on a shelf in
the back of his store for six
years.

We went outside, as it was
warm and the sun was shining. I
suggested we place Compassion on a
table, so people could gather
'round for a viewing. I brought my

trusty turntable to make the turning easier.

"Compassion is as interesting from the back as she is from the front," I said. We got a table, and the chairs around it filled right away. The media person, whose name I will not divulge as I do not have his permission to use it, brought up a logical point.

We were discussing the inability of anyone other than the individual carver to determine the age of a crystal skull, and how so many were lying for financial gain. We were laughing about some of the outlandish stories that were coming out to prove the legitimacy of some of these skulls when the media person spoke up.

"This crystal skull is so unique that it doesn't matter when it was carved or who carved it!" he pronounced. I had to agree.

"All that I report is what others have written, and it's all on my website; observations are offered by Annie or Phyllis or whomever is attending us. I rarely go to a presentation alone for this purpose, as the information needs to be authenticated." I explained.

At this time, Philip's mother-in-law and her husband arrived. She had been bedridden, but now with the help of a walker was able to get out of the car. She was in her late 80s, and feeble. I placed Compassion on a table at ground level so her mother could see her. She came to Compassion after She placed her hands on Compassion's head and closed her eyes. We were all silent. Then her husband, who was walking with a cane, came up and did the same.

Later, when we moved into the Sunlight we were all up in the higher part of the backyard, we saw Philip's mother-in-law making her way up the knoll, using only a cane. I offered her my seat, as I am always next to Compassion when showing her. She refused and started doing "stand-up comedy,n" her jokes now the center of attention!

All in all, it was an extremely enjoyable time with some truly fascinating people, from bank executive to wine merchant, to psychic -- and even a well-known media host, thrown in for good measure. I loved it! We thanked the Kathleen and Philip for their hospitality and a chance to meet her mother, father and friends. These people are as genuine and full of love.

Around this time, Philip was working on an article, which was later published in *Atlantis Rising* magazine. He and I discussed its accuracy by email, and I had a chance to review his work. My hunch proved to be correct. His reporting was unbiased, intelligent, and to the point. You can find this article at http://www.philipcoppens.com/compassion.html

Philip dismantles the claim that the Mitchell-Hedges Skull is unique in its complexity, for now, with the appearance of Compassion; it is obviously not the world's only human-size, clear quartz skull with detachable jaw.

Philip has spent a lot of time with the M. H. Skull in Scotland, so his opinion is well founded and respected. Given Compassion's three layers of quartz showing fissures on the surface, this skull could not have been made with modern grinding machines, in his opinion.

Affirming the findings of Dr. Minch, Philip noted the areas on the palate that showed hand-polishing marks that "jumped" over high areas instead of cutting through, as a grinding wheel would have done. This skull has shown to me that it was cut against the axis of the quartz crystal and over three distinctive layers. Yet regardless of its physical uniqueness and beauty, as I often say: It's what a skull *does* that determines its value. This is why I have gone to great lengths to get the written accounts of many people. They have no vested interest and speak the truth from their hearts.

All I have is this book to share with those who come to see Compassion. I hope you're enjoying it, as it's factual and deeply revealing. There may be times when I seem to be going off on a tangent, but absent much writing experience, I have simply tried to tell it like it is.

This work is a living legacy of my life with a crystal skull. I didn't ask for the responsibility but once confronted with Compassion I have had to confront my Ego and all discord it has caused me. This is coming back to me as I spend time with Compassion and those she is bringing to her. I was told: "Criticizing divides people, forgiveness unites them."

The duality of my life is changing with my daily contact with this crystal skull. Sending love, checking my automatic tendency to fall into the old trap of what I feel is right and wrong.

I seem to be doing it the hard way. I am not a medium and do not know how to channel. I cannot judge those that are chandlers when a skull is bought. This is their path and who is to say they have not suddenly been given this ability to act as an intermediary between their skull and people.

Not being so blessed and coming from an Ego centered past this has been a struggle. I have learned to accept Compassion speaks for herself.

I feel at this time to relate to the reader a very unusual finding we made when placing Compassion on a "white" light box when Annie and I first had the time to examine her. This process was told to me by others online that had crystal skulls and ask me to try.

I bought a light box large enough to support Compassion. It was about five inches square so I have to place her on the diagonal to keep her from sliding off one end.

I photographed here from various angles and when I saw the results I was shocked. First she showed a golden color. Second we were to see two faces looking back at us. One appeared to be a horse skull with a headdress the other was the profile of what I can only guess is a Baboon or monkey.

Later at the advice of another skull caretaker I used different colored filter paper the heads were again captured with a blue filter and later with green. No other colors gave us these images. I am still doing research to find

out the connection with these images to a crystal skull.
PREPARING FOR THE SHIFT

Chapter 19

Over the years I have learned, "Compassion will reach those who reach out to her." It has been such a thrill to see people light up from their first exposure to Compassion. Some grab their hearts and others hold the top of their heads; many have tears running down their cheeks. This, I am told, is an indication of the body's energy centers (or chakras) opening up. It can be a shocking moment for some. For me, the experience means I am fulfilling my destiny with Compassion.

At the time of this writing I am re-reading Patricia Corei's book *Atlantis Rising - the struggle of Darkness and Light.* I am overwhelmed with the parallel. She uses the Anniunaki is the dark forces bringing technological advances to the Atlanteans while giving them the Yang energy of the Sacred Male Ego. This is centered

hierarchical separation and the
belief in greed for money and
therefore, personal power and
control over mankind. Patricia
contends the Atlantean people had
reached a pinnacle of success in
the light of the Yin energy of
nurturing and compassion for
themselves, others and in harmony
with Gaia, the Earth.

This is what I have intuited
from my living with Compassion and
the response people have brought
to us after spending time with
this most unusual crystal skull. I
hear about Compassion representing
the Sacred Feminine energy coming
in at this time in Man  kind's
evolution.

Now, History is repeating it's
self with the extreme Yang energy
as we reach our civilization's
peak as it happened in Atlantis.

We as a world are declining
with a loss of our focus on the
energy that created us and
therefore, gave us respect to
honor ourselves and our planet.

I am learning, and I know many
are also feeling the "potential"
Yin energy coming to balance the
cycle of energies.

I have to feel this has been Compassion's message for many. She is here to fulfill her destiny once again by being a physical reminder of our Spiritual greatness. Compassion has to be seen and felt to get the message she is sending. I could write on but until one actually experiences the unconditional love I fall short with my attempt to pass this on in words.

I am no longer a hard-charging fisherman and do not need to push. As Compassion continues to open up, opportunities become abundant to share her.

I have to work on what I am sharing. It's like the "Zen of pushing by resting!" If Compassion is all about the feeling and practice of compassion, then that is where we have to be going.

This is all easy to say, but in this world of duality, belief systems make it difficult to let it all go and flow with the energy of the oneness around us.

I am still not the person I can visualize as living wholly in compassion. After reading James Redfield's popular book, *The*

*Celestine Prophecy,* I just had to see the movie. Both book and movie had a very positive effect on me. I am a visual learner, and when I saw these people learning to see things from a higher vibration, it visually actualized the concept of what the crystal skulls are here to do.

Every crystal skull has its own particular message I suppose, but ultimately it's all about "seeing things differently." In this movie, people saw the golden light around Nature, which signaled that the SHIFT had begun within them personally.

For example, one simple exercise in learning to "see" would be to search for the etheric light passing between two fingers that are almost touching. When this is accomplished easily, then looking at a flower or a tree or a person reveals them in their true light form.

They haven't changed at all; it's your perception that is changing. Your vibrational frequency has been tuned to a higher vibration. Using exercises such as this one, as well as steady self-observation, we can participate in our own evolution.

My point is we are not helpless victims on this planet. At what level we participate in creating the world is entirely up to us. Remember it's the message that the skulls are her for.

Compassion or any quartz crystal can serve as a holographic focal point for such an exercise, as it can possibly reflect back to you exactly who you are. When your own skull or crystal glows with the golden light, then you know you are on your way.

No one can do it for you, but they can get you started with a discipline. Any practice that enables you to calm your mind and not listen to the internal chatter is a good one. Having a focal point that has electrical potential, like quartz, can be particularly helpful in this regard.

I believe that the practice of contemplation and/or meditation will serve anyone, at any age. I am what is known as a baby boomer. I have the time now to reflect as I watch my grandchildren growing up. Teaching children to take a few moments a day to sit quietly, focus on a quartz object, and still their overactive minds will allow them to see the images inside with their imagination, while keeping their pure minds open. It is my hope they will carry this into adulthood.

This is our legacy. A parent can lead only by example. I feel that listening to the "small, still voice within," and seeing with clear eyes will give our children the inner strength and wisdom to take action in times of troubles, when they are alone.

When the parents model the practice of compassion, their children tend to see themselves as "guests" on their inherited Earth, rather than exploiters. They look at others with empathy, knowing there is a part of themselves out there in everything and everyone, yearning to be accepted and loved.

If our children understand this concept of compassion, it is easier for them to actualize it in their lives. They will have much work to do, and will hopefully understand that we had forgotten about compassion when we left them contaminated air, soil, and water.

I can no longer travel to show Compassion at my own expense. I suppose I've known right along that this time was coming, as I know I am not living in a perfect world.

I received an email from a lovely lady named Summer. She'd seen a photo of Compassion and, having just moved to the Ventura area, wanted to get together. We made an appointment for a personal presentation at her home.

She and her very interesting husband have a collection of crystals, many more than I have. I was very surprised indeed. They knew crystals, and had every variety. The inside of the house was wall-to-wall crystals on every flat surface.

This reminded me of my own situation when Annie finally had to ask me to make room for her to sit down! Summer's husband was studying world spiritual beliefs, and was very well educated.

We had a most illuminating visit. Summer's husband sat me down and explored the concept of

sharing. He explained that I was
not to feel guilty for taking
money from people who are willing
to share their abundance with me
in exchange for time with
Compassion. All who visit her hope
to make contact and take something
away that will make the sharing
worthwhile. The view of sharing
takes the guilt away, and balances
the time and expense of showing
Compassion. The expectation is
that each individual will be
enriched by the experience.

We agreed to meet again at my
Lemurian Sanctuary. This is a very
private place for me, and I do not
share it with anyone. However,
these people were tuned into
Compassion and are higher-
vibrational souls.

After this first meeting, I
meditated with Compassion, hoping
to receive intuitions from her, as
that is how we'd communicated thus
far. It was very interesting, as I
was made to feel comfortable with
these new ideas, and also felt the
familiar unconditional love that
has come to most people in her
presence.

The compromise for me was asking for a sharing donation to keep my travels with Compassion on the road. I surrendered this position to the Universe and felt relieved. Summer and I talked online, and made an appointment to share the Lemurian Sanctuary.

What I have learned is to be aware of my deepest intentions for Compassion, as Jane had instructed back in Tempe. She warned me that Compassion would be coming from my heart, and if it weren't pure in service to Mankind I would suffer when Compassion totally activates.

My work will begin in earnest after 2012 so I was told back in 2009. To help those that are confused and troubled after the Shift. It is said we may have to move into our light bodies to make this transition; I don't know in my position I am following the information given to me as one to be left behind for this work.

If Compassion touches you with her message of the Sacred Feminine, take it to others and be the shinning light of unconditional love. Start by becoming the person you are

talking to because there is a part
of you in them. Give them the love
and nurturing your want. The
change will be manifest in you. If
you are troubled and lost the
crystal skull Compassion will be
here.


The End

ABOUT THE AUTHOR

Joseph Bennett is a career mariner, joined Navy in 1964. Worked as Hospital Corpsman in surgery aboard the USS TICONDEROGA CVA 14. Honorably discharged in 1969.

Homesteaded at the head of Kachemak Bay, Homer, Alaska. Commercial fished Herring, King Crab and Salmon for 24 years..

Restored a 1958 wood sailboat then sailed back to Alaska. Sailboat was inspected for charter out of Homer, Alaska in 1985 for 24 passengers, 20 miles offshore.

Exxon oil spill ended fishing and charter business in 1989.

He sold his fishing business sailed the wood boat to Monterey and then to San Diego for the 1992 America's Cup. He later bought, restored and sailed a 1972 Columbia 50 sailboat 6000 miles along California's coast from 1993 to present where Annie and he still living onboard.

Bibliography:

*The Skull Speaks* and *The Veil of Time*.
Carole Davis, coauthor with Brian Hadley-James

*Atlantis in America Navigators of the Ancient World*.
Ivar Zapp and George Erikson

*Dying into Freedom*, Susan C. Storch, Rn, Ma.

*The Celestine Prophecy*, James Redfield

*Atlantis Rising, The struggle of Darkness and Light, Patricia Corey*

Made in the USA
Charleston, SC
15 January 2012